Monumental Heritage of Mandi

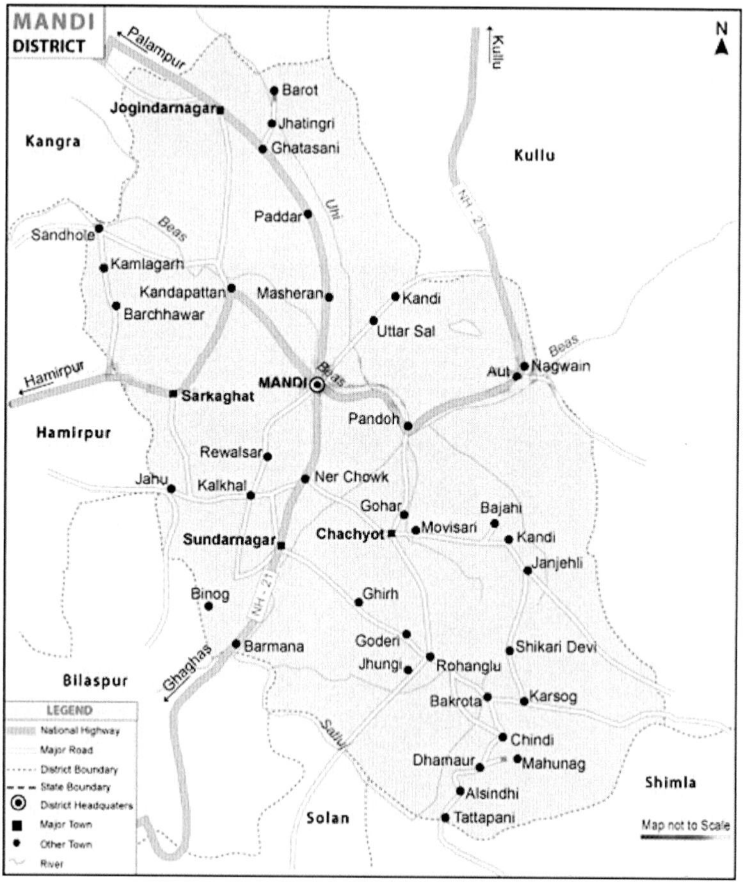
MANDI
DISTRICT
Palampur
Kullu
N
Barot
Jogindarnagar
Jhatingri
Ghatasani
Kangra
Kullu
Paddar
Uhl
Sandhole
Beas
Kamlagarh
Kandapattan
Masheran
Kandi
Barchhawar
Uttar Sal
Beas
Hamirpur
MANDI
Beas
Aut
Nagwain
Sarkaghat
Pandoh
NH - 21
Hamirpur
Rewalsar
Jahu
Kalkhal
Ner Chowk
Gohar
Bajahi
Sundarnagar
Chachyot
Movisari
Kandi
Janjehli
Binog
NH - 21
Ghirh
Barmana
Goderi
Shikari Devi
Jhungi
Rohanglu
Ghaghas
Bilaspur
Bakrota
Karsog
Satluj
Chindi
Dhamaur
Mahunag
Alsindhi
Shimla
Solan
Tattapani
Map not to Scale
LEGEND
National Highway
Major Road
District Boundary
State Boundary
District Headquaters
Major Town
Other Town
River

Map of Mandi

Monumental Heritage of Mandi

A Brief Introduction

B.M. Pande

C. Dorje

Kaveri Books

New Delhi - 110002

ISBN : 978-81-7479-231-0
First Published in 2021

Published by
Kaveri Books
4832/24, Ansari Road, Daryaganj,
New Delhi - 110 002 (India)
Ph. : 011- 4707 2321
E-mail : info@kaveribooks.com
kaveribooks@gmail.com
Website : www.kaveribooks.com

Typesetting at Creative Graphics, Delhi

PRINTED IN INDIA

Preface

The historic town of Mandi in Himachal Pradesh was the capital of the erstwhile Mandi State which was set up by Raja Ajbar Sen in the year 1527 CE. He was the first great ruler of Mandi who assumed the designation of Raja. Published historical literature refers that in ancient times Mandi was an important trade and commercial centre between Indian plains and Ladakh, Yarkand and Central Asia. Mandi is also known for its old temples with their enormous range of exquisite carvings thereby earning the title of 'Varanasi of the Hills' or 'Chhoti Kashi of Himachal'. Mostly dedicated to Shiva and the Shakti, these temples are built around a sunken garden and also along the Beas and Suketi river front. Old bazaars, and exquisitely carved stone temples attract the eyes of any beholder and its surroundings present a panoramic view of the town. This one-time capital of the princely state is a developing town that still retains much of its original charm and character.

In the present monograph an attempt has been made to describe the monumental heritage which has been preserved by the local inhabitants of the area for centuries. It is hoped that this will serve as a guide for serious scholars to carry out detailed research in the respective field on the one hand and would be found useful by visitors particularly the tourists during their visit to the town on the other. A brief introduction of Mandi has been given in the first chapter while the historical background of the erstwhile Mandi State has been briefly described in the second chapter. The details of the monumental heritage of Mandi have been given in the third chapter.

This work does not claim to be in-depth study but only outlines the basic information about the town and its varied monuments illustrated by way of photographs and line-drawings. We have retained the name(s) of the temples and deities as pronounced by the local people rather than Sanskritizing names of the deities.

It is hoped that it will serve the purpose of both scholars and lay visitors to the town. At the same time, it may also kindle the desire in the inhabitants of this great town to know more about their heritage and to put in their efforts in preserving it.

Mr. Rakesh Goel of Kaveri Books deserve appreciation for taking up the publication of this monograph in record time.

B.M. Pande

C. Dorje

Contents

Preface	v
List of Figures	viii
List of Plates	ix
1. General Information	1
2. Historical Background of Mandi State	8
3. Monumental Remains of Mandi	29
(A) Shaiva Shrines	
(B) Shakti or Devi Shrines	
(C) Vaishnava Shrines	
(D) Miscellaneous Shrines	
(E) Other Monuments	
Bibliography	144
Index	147

List of Figures

Fig. 1 (a-d) : Bhutnatha Temple, Mandi
Fig. 2 (a-c) : Panchavaktra Temple, Mandi
Fig. 3 (a-b) : Ardhanarishvara temple, Mandi
Fig. 4 (a-c) : Shiva-Deula (Bijali Mahadeva) Temple, Mandi
Fig. 5 (a-c) : Ekadasharudra Temple, Mandi
Fig. 6 (a-c) : Siddh-Bhadra Temple, Mandi
Fig. 7 (a-c) : Shiva-Rudra Temple, Mandi
Fig. 8 (a-c) : Mahadeva Temple, Mandi
Fig. 9 (a-c) : Mahamrityunjay Temple, Mandi
Fig. 10 (a-c) : Raneshvara Mahadeva Temple, Mandi
Fig. 11 (a-c) : Neelakantha Mahadeva Temple, Mandi
Fig. 12 (a-c) : Ramalingeshvara Mahadeva Temple, Mandi
Fig. 13 (a-c) : Mahadeva Neelkantha Temple, Mandi
Fig. 14 (a-c) : Shiva Temple, Chhota Tarna
Fig. 15 (a-c) : Shiva Temple, Mandi
Fig. 16 (a-b) : Siddh-Shambu and Siddh-Kali Temple
Fig. 17 (a-c) : Shiva Temple, Mandi
Fig. 18 (a-c) : Dugleshvara Mahadeva Temple, Mandi
Fig. 19 (a-b) : Mahakala Temple, Mandi
Fig. 20 (a-c) : Sitala Mata Temple, Mandi
Fig. 21 (a-b) : Mata Chintapurni Temple, Mandi
Fig. 22 (a-b) : Durga Maheshvara MahadevaTemple, Mandi
Fig. 23 (a-b) : Bhuvaneshvari Devi Temple, Mandi
Fig. 24 (a-b) : Jwala Mata Temple, Mandi
Fig. 25 (a-c) : Jalpa Mata Temple, Paddal, Mandi
Fig. 26 (a-c) : Jalpa Devi Temple, Mandi
Fig. 27 (a-b) : Bangleshvari Mahadeva Temple, Mandi
Fig. 28 (a-b) : Shyama-Kali Temple, Tarana Hills
Fig. 29 (a-b) : Bhimakali Temple, Mandi
Fig. 30 (a-c) : Radha-Krishna Temple, Purani Mandi
Fig. 31 (a-c) : Sita-Rama Radha-Krishna Temple, Mandi
Fig. 32 (a-b) : Sanatan Dharam Sabha, Mandi
Fig. 33 (a-b) : Baba Balakrupi Temple, Mandi

List of Plates

Plate 1-2 : Bhutnatha Temple, Mandi
Plate 3-6 : Trilokinatha Temple, Mandi
Plate 7-8 : Panchavaktra Temple, Mandi
Plate 9 : Ardhanarishvara Temple, Mandi
Plate 10-11 : Shiva-Deula (Bijali-Mahadeva) Temple, Mandi
Plate 12-13 : Ekadasharudra Temple, Mandi
Plate 14-15 : Stone Sculptures and rock-cut Shiva-lingas
Plate 16-17 : Siddh Bhadra Temple, Mandi
Plate 18 : Shiva-Rudra Temple, Mandi
Plate 19 : Mahadeva Temple, Mandi
Plate 20-21 : Mahamrityunjaya Temple, Mandi
Plate 22-23 : Raneshvara Mahadeva Temple, Mandi
Plate 24 : Neelakantha Mahadeva Temple, Mandi
Plate 25-26 : Ramaligeshvara Mahadeva Temple, Mandi
Plate 27-28 : Mahadeva Neelakantha Temple, Mandi
Plate 29 : Shiva Temple, Mandi
Plate 30 : Shiva and Shani Temples, Mandi
Plate 31-32 : Siddh Shambhu and Siddh Kali Temples, Mandi
Plate 33 : Standing image of Siddha Bhairava
Plate 34-35 : Shiva Temple, Mandi
Plate 36-37 : Dugleshvara Mahadeva Temple, Mandi
Plate 38-39 : Monolithic rock-cut shrine, Mandi
Plate 40-41 : Siddh-Shambhu rock-cut sculptures, Mandi
Plate 42-44 : Mahakala Temple, Mandi
Plate 45 : Kameshvara Mahadeva Temple, Mandi
Plate 46-47 : Sitala Mata Temple, Mandi
Plate 48 : Durga Maheshvara Mahadeva Temple, Mandi
Plate 49 : Bhuvaneshvari Devi Temple, Mandi
Plate 50-51 : Jwala Mata Temple, Mandi
Plate 52-53 : Jalpa Mata Temple, Mandi
Plate 54 : Shyama Kali Temple, Mandi
Plate 55-56 : Bhimakali Temple, Mandi
Plate 57-59 : Chamunda Mata Temple, Mandi

Plate 60 : Radha-Krishna Temple, Mandi
Plate 61-62 : Jagannatha Temple, Mandi
Plate 63 : Sanatan Dharam Sabha, Mandi
Plate 64-65 : Baba Balakrupi Temple, Mandi
Plate 66-67 : Siddha Ganapati Temple, Mandi
Plate 68-69 : Barsela monuments, Mandi
Plate 70-71 : Mandi Palace, side view
Plate 72-75 : Baolis at different locations in Mandi
Plate 76 : Anglo-Vernacular School Building
Plate 77 : Heritage Bridge, Mandi

1

General Information

The present day Himachal Pradesh, according to the *Mahabharata* comprised of number of *Janapadas or* small republics, each of which constituted both a state and a cultural unit. The *Audumbaras* were the most prominent among the ancient tribes of Himachal who lived in the lower hills between Pathankot and Jwalamukhi. Believed to have been an independent republic *Trigarta* lay in the foothills drained by three rivers, i.e. the Ravi, Beas and Satluj and hence the name. The kingdom of Kuluta was situated in the upper Beas valley, also known as the Kullu valley. Its capital was Naggar. The kingdom of the *Kunindas* covered the area lying between the Beas, Satluj and Yamuna rivers, i.e. the Shimla and Sirmour hills. Their administration resembled a republic with members of a central assembly sharing the powers of the king. Chandragupta Maurya gradually subdued most of the republics though he did not rule over them directly. Ashoka, the grandson of Chandragupta, extended his boundaries to the Himalayan region. He built many stupas, one of which was in the Kullu valley. After the collapse of the Gupta Empire and before the rise of Harsha, this area was again ruled by petty chiefs known as Thakurs and Ranas. With the rise of Harsha (606-647 CE) in the early seventh century, most of these small states acknowledged his overall supremacy though many local powers remained with the petty chiefs. A few decades after Harsha's death

(647 CE), many Rajput states came up in Rajasthan and Indus plains. They fought amongst themselves and those vanquished moved to the hills with their followers, where they set up small states or principalities. These states were Kangra, Nurpur, Suket, Mandi, Kutlehar, Baghal, Bilaspur, Nalagarh, Keonthal, Dhami, Kunihar, Bushahar and Sirmour.

These small hill states enjoyed a large degree of independence till the eve of Muslim invasions in northern India. States in the foothills were devastated by Muslim invaders from time to time. Mahmud Ghazni conquered Kangra at the beginning of the tenth century. Timur and Sikandar Lodi also marched through the lower hills and captured several forts and fought many battles. Later on, as the Mughal dynasty began to break up, the rulers of the hill states took full advantage. The Katoch rulers of Kangra availed of this opportunity and Kangra regained independence under Maharaja Sansar Chand who ruled for nearly half a century. After he took formal possession of Kangra fort, Sansar Chand began to expand his territory. The states of Chamba, Suket, Mandi, Bilaspur, Guler, Jaswan, Siwan and Datarpur came under the direct or indirect control of Sansar Chand. The Gorkhas, came to power in Nepal in the year 1768 and consolidated militarily and began to expand their territory. Sirmour and Shimla hill states were annexed by the Gorkhas and under Amar Singh Thapa, Kangra was under siege. He managed to defeat Sansar Chand, the ruler of Kangra in 1806, but the Gorkhas could not capture the Kangra fort. In 1809, Kangra came under the control of Maharaja Ranjit Singh. After this defeat the Gorkhas began to expand towards south. This resulted in the Anglo-Gorkha war. They came into direct conflict with the British along the Tarai belt and the Gorkhas were expelled from the hill states. Thus the British slowly emerged as the paramount power in this tract. After the Anglo-Gorkha war, the common border of the British domain and Punjab became very sensitive. Both the Sikhs and the British wanted to avoid direct conflict, but after the death of Ranjit Singh, the Khalsa army fought a number of wars with the British. In 1845, when the Sikhs invaded the British territory by crossing the Satluj, the rulers of many hill states sided with the English as they were looking for an opportunity to settle scores with the former. Many of these rulers entered into secret communication with the English. After the first Anglo-Sikh war, the British did not restore the hill territory vacated by Sikhs to their original owners. The revolt in 1857 or the first Indian War of Independence was the result of the building up of political, social, economic, religious and military grievances against the British. People of the hill states were not as politically alive as the people in other parts of the country. They remained more or less aloof and so did their rulers with the exception of Bushahar. Some of them even rendered help to the British during the revolt. Among them were the rulers of Chamba, Bilaspur, Bhagal and Dhami. The rulers of Bushahar acted in a manner hostile to the interests of British. However, it is not clear whether they actually aided the rebels or not. The British territories in the hills came under the British Crown after Queen Victoria's proclamation in 1858. The states of Chamba, Mandi and Bilaspur made good progress in many fields during the British rule. During the First World War, virtually all rulers of the hill states remained loyal and contributed to the British war effort both in the form of men and material. Amongst these were the states of Kangra, Siba, Nurpur, Chamba, Suket, Mandi and Bilaspur.

The people of the hills also participated in the freedom struggle. The highlights of the freedom movement in this tract including Praja Mandal launched agitation against the British yoke in areas under direct British Rule. In other princely states, agitations were launched for social and political reforms. However these were directed more against the princes than against the British and as such were mere extensions of the freedom movement.

During 1906, Mandi was also visited by Lala Lajpat Rai for organizing revolutionary activities. Hardev Ram joined the revolutionary band of patriots in 1913 and visited Shanghai, America and Japan where he met Lala Hardayal and Dr. Mathura Singh. Another revolutionary of Mandi, Bhai Hirda Ram started participating in revolutionary activities in 1914. He joined Ras Behari Bose, Sant Baba Wasakha Singh Dadehar, Mathura Singh, Kartar Singh Sarba, Bhai Parma Nand and Moropant Pingle.The Mandi conspiracy was carried out in 1914-15 under the influence of the Ghadar party. Meetings were held in Mandi and Suket states in December 1914 and January 1915 and it was decided to murder the Superintendent and Wazir of Mandi and Suket, to loot the treasury, blow up the bridge over the Beas River. However, the conspirators were caught and sentenced to long terms in prison. The Pajhota agitation in which the people of a part of Sirmour state revolted is regarded as an extension of the Quit India Movement of 1942. The Chief Commissioner's province of Himachal Pradesh came into being on 15th April, 1948. With the implementation of the Constitution of India, Himachal Pradesh became a Part C State on 26th January, 1950 and was declared as a Union Territory on 1st November, 1956.

On 18th December, 1970 the Parliament passed the State of Himachal Pradesh Act and on 25th January 1971, it emerged as the eighteenth state of the Indian Union. Thus, Himachal Pradesh has come a long way since then. It has seen a number of full-fledged governments which have led the State towards economic self-reliance.

The present district Mandi was formed with the merger of two princely States of Mandi and Suket on 15th April 1948, when Himachal Pradesh came into existence. Ever since the formation of the district, it has not witnessd any changes in its jurisdiction. Under the jurisdiction of Mandi district, there are seven tehsils Jogindernagar, Sundernagar, Chachyot, Thunag, Karsog, Sarkaghat, Sadar-Mandi and nine Sub-Tehsils, i.e., Ladbharol, Padher, Sandhole, Dharmpur, Baldwara, Nihri, Kotti, Aut, Balichowki. Mandi is the Zonal Headquartres of Central Zone covering the districts of Bilaspur, Hamirpur, Kullu and Mandi itself and has gained much importance from administrative point of view.

Mandi district (latitude 31^0 13' 50" and 32^0 04' 30 "North and longitude 76^0 37' 20" and 77^0 23' 15" East) is bound by Kangra on the north-west, Hamirpur and Bilaspur in the west, Arki tehsil of Solan district in the south, Shimla district in the south-west and Kullu district in the east.The greater part of the district is hilly terrain with the main ranges of hills running from the north to the south. The Jalori range divides the watershed of the Satluj and the Beas. Its northern slopes are unusually well wooded with deodar and blue pine forests. The highest peak in the range is Shikari Devi (11,060 feet), crowned by the shrine of a local goddess. The range has three main spurs which extend throughout the tract known as the Mandi Saraj. The Sikandar Range commences from the tri-junction with Suket and Bilaspur. To the north of the Beas is the Nargu Range, a continuation of the Bir Bangahal, separating Mandi from Kullu proper and crossed by the Bhubu pass (9,480 feet). In the centre of the district is the Ghoghar-ki-Dhar, the slopes of which contain the salt quarries of Darang and Gumman.

Two main rivers are the Beas and the Satluj and the other principal tributaries of the Beas on the north bank are the Uhl, Luni, Rana and Binu and on the south bank are the Hanse, Tirthan, Bakhli, Jiuni, Suketi, Ranodi, Son and Bakar. Several of the valleys are open and are often irrigable from *kuhls*, small water channels, and contain some of the most fertile land in the State. Due to the hilly terrain, some of the hills are so precipitous that cultivation in large scale is impossible. The unused land is covered with forests and the grassy slopes for grazing the herds of cattle.

As far as the climatic conditions of Mandi is concerned, it is hot in summers and cold in winters and temperature varies during summer between 18.9°C (66.02°F) and 39.6°C (103.28°F) and in winter 6.7°C (44.06°F) and 26.2°C (79.16°F). Monthly precipitation also varies between 25.4 mm in November to 228.6 mm in August. The average total annual precipitation is 832 mm. Mandi generally experiences rainfall during end of summer season.Mandi is also located in Seismic Zone IV near a fault line and is prone to earthquakes.

Mandi, formerly known as Mandav Nagar, has its roots in the great sage Rishi 'Mandav' who is believed to have prayed in this area. The name may have been derived from the common word *mandi* which means "market" and also connected with the Sanskrit root *mandapika* meaning "an open hall or shed". Mandav Nagar was its official name until it was changed to Mandi, and is now the most widely used name for the city. Mandi is also known by the name of Zahor, and is associated with Padmasambhava (750-800 CE). The place is still visited by Buddhist pilgrims from Tibet, Ladakh, Spiti, Kinnaur and Lahaul; Padmasambhava is believed to reside on the floating islands in the lake of Rewalsar. However, Hindus look upon the sacred Rewalsar as the abode of Lomasa Rishi. It is situated on an average altitude of 1,044 metres on the left bank of the river Beas near its junction with the Suketi Nala. Mandi wears an impressive appearance with mountains providing an excellent backdrop and is easily accessible by road. Mandi town is a bowl-shaped tableland on the banks of the river Beas, surrounded by the high hill ranges of Gandharv Hills, Motipur Dhar, Rehra Dhar and Tarna Hill. Two small rivulets, Suketi Khad and Skodhi Khad join the river Beas and the town is built on the banks of the Beas river at the confluence.

Mandi, the headquarters of the district, is also known for ancient stone shrines with range of fine carvings and remains of old historical buildings and palaces. As such the town is often referred to as "Chhoti Kashi" or "Varanasi of Hills" or "Kashi of Hills", etc.

The present town is well connected with the state capital, Shimla at a distance of 153 km, Pathankot at a distance of 228 km and Chandigarh which is approximately 200 km. The alternative to reach Mandi from Delhi is to travel by train upto Kiratpur Sahib and Rupnagar. All the buses going from Delhi and Chandigarh to Mandi have to pass through Rupnagar and Kiratpur. The nearest railway station currently is Jogindernagar almost 50 km away from the city. The nearest airport is Kullu Airport at Bhuntar which is at a distance of about 65 km from Mandi town.

Mandi is widely known for the international Shivaratri festival, held for seven days in the month of *Phalguna* (February-March) every year. This celebration is said to have started in the year 1526 to commemorate the foundation of the town. On the Shivaratri day, a colourful procession is taken out. Madho Rai, the presiding deity, leads the procession and was followed by the Raja during the State times and by the high dignitaries after Independence. This procession is preceded by a party of musicians who play on the traditional music instruments. The gods and goddesses and deities are brought to this place from various parts of the district to pay homage to Madho Rai. The dancing devotees and other hill folks in their colourful dresses follow this procession which terminates at Paddal ground. Various cultural programmes are also arranged during the nights where parties from various parts of the country as well as outside used to present their performances.

2
Historical Background of Mandi State*

Early history of Mandi is very hazy and the only place that finds mention is Rewalsar in the *Skanda Purana* where it is called as a sacred place of pilgrimage. There is also a legend that the present village Karanpur is said to have been founded by Karna, a hero of the *Mahabharata*. The temple at Guma points to the locality where the Pandavas are said to have taken shelter when attempt to burn them down failed. Beyond these stray references, not much information is available about Mandi in early literature. According to the Tibetan tradition, Padmasambhava (750-800 CE), the great Buddhist patriarch, who was summoned by king Khrisong-detsen of Tibet and is credited with the introduction of Buddhism in Tibet hailed from Zahor. On the basis of this it has been concluded that Mandi must have been a great place of Buddhist learning about this time. It is also said that Mandi provided a safe home not only for persecuted Buddhists at the hands of King Langdharma (900 CE), but also for their religious books which were carried by them and deposited somewhere in the State. The earliest mention of the town is in an inscription in the Trilokinatha temple which is dated in the year 2164 of the Kali era and Saka year 1442, corresponding to 1520 CE. The reigning

---

* Based on *The Gazetteer of India, Mandi district, 1920; History of the Panjab Hill States,* Volume II by J. Hutchison & J.Ph. Vogel, Lahore, 1933 and *History of Mandi State* by Man Mohan, 1930.

families of Mandi and Suket are said to be from a common progenitor of the *Chandravansi* line of *kshatriyas* who claim their descent from the Pandavas of the *Mahabharata*. The genealogy preserved in the state speaks of some 161 rulers before Bir Sen, the progenitor of the local dynasty, moved on to settle in the Punjab hills. The State of Suket is said to have been founded by Bir Sen (765 CE), an ancestor of the Sena Dynasty of Bengal. The then reigning Chief Sahu Sen had a quarrel with his younger brother Bahu Sen, who left Suket to seek his fortunes elsewhere. The separation of Mandi from Suket took place about the year 1200 CE. Bahu Sen after leaving Suket settled at Mangalor in Kullu and is said to have acquired territory there and was recognized as a Rana or local chief. He was followed by nine chiefs of whom the names of Nirmata Sen, Naravahan Sen, Kanavahana Sen, Survahana Sen, Vira Sen, Samundra Sen, Keshabana Sen, Mangal Sen and Jaya Sen only have been preserved.

Karenchana Sen (1278 CE) was tenth in descent from Bahu Sen and his *rani* was the daughter of the Rana of Seokot. He invaded and conquered the adjoining tracts of Panjain and annexed Thujari and Kao. He subdued the Ranas of Bans, Ner and Bagi Thach and forced them to pay tribute. Then the chief, Karenchan Sen was killed fighting against the Kullu Raja; his *rani*, who was pregnant at that time, fled alone to her father who was the chief of Seokot, who had no son. Here she gave birth to a baby boy who was named Ban, the tree under which he was born. Ban had hardly crossed the age of 15 when he defeated the chief of Kelti who used to plunder travellers. On the death of the chief of Seokot, Ban succeeded to the chiefship of Seokot. He killed the Rana of Sakor and took posesssion of his lands. He also built the Parashar temple. He then changed his residence to Bhiun on the right bank of the Beas, some distance away from the present Mandi town. After reigning for about 45 years, he died in the year 1304 CE and was succedeed by his son Kalyan Sen, who acquired a piece of land on the right bank of the Beas, Batahuli, the old Mandi and developed as his capital which continued to be for about a century and half. The area around Kelti, Chaheti and Samur was annexed and the Rana of Sagrur was killed and his territory annexed. He died in 1332 CE and was succeeded by his son, Hira Sen. The area around Kanhwal was annexed but Hira Sen was killed by the Rana of Gandharb in the struggle in 1360 CE. He was succeeded by his younger brother, Dhratri Sen who died without any issue. He was succeeded by his uncle Narendra Sen in 1400 CE followed by Harjai Sen (1440 CE) and Dilawar Sen (1470 CE). It was in the reign of latter that Sikandar Lodi attacked Mandi and his garrison remained in the hills for about nine years. After the demise of Dilawar Sen in 1499 CE, Ajbar Sen took over the reign of Mandi State.

Ajbar Sen (1500 CE) was nineteenth in descent from Bahu Sen. He established a new Mandi town in 1527 CE as the capital of the state, and is the headquarters of the present district. Mandi emerged as a separate state in the beginning of the sixteenth century. The earliest mention of the name Mandi occurs in the Trilokinatha temple inscription dated 1442 of Saka era (corresponding to 1520 CE). Ajbar Sen was the first great ruler of Mandi who assumed the title of Raja. He was probably the first person to assume the designation of Raja. He consolidated the territories that he had inherited and added to them new ones that he wrested from the hands of his neighbours. The united forces of Ranas and Thakurs of Maratu, Kanhwal and Gandharb were defeated and the Rana of Gandharb was killed. The Ranas of Kamlah and Kalar States became his subject and some of the Ranas surrendered their possessions and others became tributaries by paying *mangni* partly in cash and partly in kind. He also built the old palace with four towers, now known as Chauki. The temple of Bhutanatha was built in the middle of the town and that of Trilokinatha by his Rani Suratrana or Sultana Devi. Ajbar Sen ruled for about 35 years and died in the year 1534 CE and was succeeded by Chhatar Sen (1534 CE), his eldest son, but during his reign nothing special seems to have occurred. It is said that Ajbar Sen's grandson Sahib Sen (1554 CE) followed him and ruled for 26 years while some mention that he ruled for 20 years. His Rani Prakash Dei, daughter of the Raja of Kahlur (Bilaspur) exerted great influence on him. He acquired the salt mine at Darang by driving away the Rana of Darang. He is said to have assisted Raja Jagat Singh of Kullu in the attack on the Raja of Lag in Kullu and received the territory of Saraj Mandi in lieu. He attacked the Ranas of Langot, Nabota, Biarner and Kota and subdued them all. While Sahib Sen was busy in extending his territory his wife was busy in acquiring religious merit by building tanks and drinking fountains, laying mule tracks, etc., and gave generously to the Brahmins. Her own desire was to have a son and when at last a son was born to her and was named Narayan Sen after the god Narayan Deo of Hurang. Narayan Sen (1575 CE) succeeded Sahib Sen. He continued the extension of his territory by subduing the Ranas of Ner, Pandoh and Chuhar and annexing to the state seven *garhs* or *ilaqas* of Chuhar and five *garhs* of Pandoh and large portions of Suket from Udai Sen and also fixed the boundary at Bahl and Loharu. He built the fort of Narayangarh.

It is said that he died of paralysis in about 1594 CE and was succeeded by his younger brother Keshab Sen (1595 CE). Not much is known about his reign but his only memorial for posterity is his Barsela monument which his successor raised in his honour. The memorial is the oldest of the later group. He ruled for 30 years till his death in 1623 CE and his son Hari Sen succeeded him. During his reign the Mughal hold on Mandi was tightened and Raja Jagat Singh of Nurpur was appointed Faujdar of Kangra. Jagat Singh wanted to assert the Mughal supremacy over the hill chiefs and thus increased his own power and influence. He attacked Chamba in 1623 and assassinated the regent Janardhan. His son Prithivi Singh, next in succession, took refuge in Mandi and remained there till 1642 when Raja Raj Rup, son of Jagat Singh, who was then acting as the Faujdar of Kangra, rebelled. Prithivi Singh thereupon marched on Chamba with the help of Raja of Mandi. Raja Hari Sen died in 1637 CE as recorded on his Barsela monument on the left bank of the Suketi Khad. He was succeeded by his minor son, Suraj Sen and the state administration was looked after by Karoria Khatri. He was an ambitious ruler, but he could not extend his territory on account of Mughal supremacy and Mandi as well as the other Hill states because tributaries of the Mughal empire. An attempt was made by Raja Jagat Singh of Nurpur to annex Mandi by means of treachery by arranging marriage of his daughter with Suraj Sen so as to get an opportunity to assassinate his son-in-law during the marriage festivities at Nurpur. He went to Nurpur and some of the marriage ceremonies were duly performed. He received a hint from Jagat Singh's Rani secretly about the proposal and he unceremoniously left his bride in paternal care and escaped from Nurpur. After some time Jagat Singh and Suraj Sen were reconciled to each other and the bride arrived at Mandi and was well received by the Raja.

Raja Suraj Sen sought to enlarge his boundaries towards north and made an attack on the Raja of Bangahal but he was defeated by the combined forces of the Raja of Kullu and

Bangahal. The forts of Karanpur, Shahpur and Shamsherpur were captured by the Raja of Kullu. He tried again to recover the lost area by invading Kullu, but was again defeated resulting in the loss of salt mines of Darang and Gumman which fell into the enemy's hands. Suraj Sen was unsuccessful in his srtruggle with Man Singh, the Raja of Guler, who twice sacked Mandi and held possession of Kalar in which was situated the fort of Kamlahgarh. He occupied a high place in Mughal hierarchy and was known to be the bravest among the hill chiefs of the time. In the year 1653 Suraj Sen captured the fortress of Patri and occupied Kot Sulhani from Raja Ram Sen of Suket. He was also successful in fighting against the minor hill chiefs, particularly the Ranas of Gumman and Ner. He had eighteen sons and his only daughter was married to Hari Deo of Jammu. Unfortunately all his sons died in his life-time, and despairing of an heir he made a silver image of Vishnu, named Madho Rai in 1648 CE and assigned the State to the deity which is still the object of highest veneration by the people of the Mandi and the royal family. It is Madho Rai too who gives Raj Tilak to every ruler of Mandi. The inscription engraved on the silver image states that :

> "Surya Sen, the lord of the earth, and destroyer of his rivals, had this blameless image of the blessed discus bearer and master of all the gods, the illustrious Madho Rai which was made by Bhima, the goldsmith, in the year 1705, on Thursday, the 15th Phagan".

This date corresponds to March, 1648 CE. He built Damdama Palace and a temple in honour of Naina Devi near Riwalsar which was damaged during 1905 earthquake in the area. Suraj Sen died on the 15th of *Phagan*, 1721 (1664 CE) after ruling for 27 years. There is a pathetic story about his funeral and it is said that while Suraj Sen's *ranis* prepared themselves for the last rites of *sati* they sent messenger to the treasury for money to be given in charity, but found that the officials of the state had put all the valuables under lock and key. In their vexation and disappointment one of the *ranis*, Parkash Dei threw her dagger at the wall of the Damdama Palace and uttered the following curse; *"Mandi Kolsara Haramkhor ki Paraul"* meaning Mandi will always be in the hands of faithless and disloyal servants. It is said that ten *ranis* committed *sati* on his death. He was succeeded by his younger brother, Shyam Sen (1664 CE) and his reign was not a long one. Shyam Sen retained the old officials and carried on the administration through them. But he was pleasure loving and extremely fond of music. Within a year of his accession, Shyam Sen attacked the territory of the Raja of Kullu and annexed the fortress of Dhanjugarh and again captured Sanaurgarh and Bajaura. Shortly afterwords, the Mughal army invaded Kahlur (Bilaspur) and the Raja of Kahlur appealed to Shyam Sen for help, which was at once given and there was considerable loss. Shyam Sen granted land in freehold to the families of all who had fallen in the campaign. He marched with a strong detachment towards Suket territories and after a furious onslaught captured a portion of Bahl. The Lohara *ilaqa* was annexed to Mandi. The boundary between the Suket and Mandi states was fixed somewhere near Dhode. On his return he built the famous Shyama Kali temple on the hill adjoining Mandi town and a fair is held every year in the month of *Asauj* (September-October) for nine days. He also built a tank across the Beas to which every infant of the Raja is taken on the eighth day of its birth. He attacked Nachan with a strong force and the Rana was made prisoner.

Shyam Sen died on the 14th of *Asauj* 1736 (1679 CE) and was succeeded by his son, Gur Sen. He took the reign of administration in his own hands and continued the work of conquest initiated earlier by his father with the assistance of Raja of Kahlur. He conquered and annexed the *garhs* or districts of Dhanyara, Bera and Patri from Suket. He visited the holy places including Jagannatha Puri and brought an image and enshrined it in a temple on the Paddal Maidan. It is said that in his reign or that of his successor, Sidh Sen, Raja Man Singh of Kullu retook some forts in Chuhar. At the battle of Dhalpur, the Raja of Kullu was defeated and was compelled to give an undertaking that he will not encroach on Mandi territory again and to pay Rupees two lakh in cash as expenses of the war. A dagger was presented to Gur Sen. Bajaura was fixed as the boundary between the two states. He reigned only for five years and died in 1684 CE.

Sidh Sen was succeeded by Raja Gur Sen; he was great warrior and added large territories to the state at the expense of Bangahal, Suket and Kullu. Mian Jappu, an illegitimate brother of Raja Gur Sen was the Wazir of the state and was a man of great ability. The administration was in his hands and he introduced the revenue system which remained in force till the Regular Settlement in 1917 by framing rules restricting expenditure which a Hindu incurs in connection with births and death, betrothal and wedding, state loans from state stores, etc. Mandi had never been so powerful prior to his reign nor after that. Mian Bir Singh, a gallant soldier, was made head of the army and launched a series of wars with a view to winning glory and fame. He captured large areas from the adjoining places. Soon after his accession Halti was captured and married the daughters of Mian Abhat Chand and Mian Jai Ram with his son Shiv Jawala Sen. In the year 1688, he acquired the forts of Nachani and Machrot and annexed Ladh and Daled. In 1690, his forces captured the forts of Dhanesargarh and some villages of Kamlah

Kot, Naraingarh and killed the Ranas. In 1698 CE Raipur was taken from Suket and Madhopur in the following year. Chhota Bangahal and a large portion of territory north of the Beas at the head of the Ravi valley of the Bangahal state was also added to Mandi. Sidh Sen invited Prithi Pal, the Raja of Bangahal to Mandi on the pretext of seeking his assistance against Suket and was received with all honour, but within a month he was imprisoned for sometime at Damdama Palace and later murdered. His head was buried in the middle of the Sidhsar tank in front of the palace and his legs and arms in the four corners of the tank where a light is kept burning every night. It was during his reign that Guru Gobind Singh, the tenth guru of the Sikhs visited Mandi towards the close of the seventeenth century. Raja Sidh Sen, who is also considered to be possessing great miraculous powers, entertained him with great hospitality and escorted him up to the state boundary. To commemorate the visit and on his request, Guru laid the foundation stone of the fortress Gurukot some twenty miles away from Mandi and the Raja requested for an assurance from the Guru that his capital would never be occupied by an enemy. Thereupon the Guru uttered.

"Mandi ko jab lutenge, asmani gole chhutenge"
(When anyone sacks Mandi, heavenly cannons will be fired).

He built the great Sairi-tank in front of the palace and also the temples of Siddh-Ganesha, Panchavaktra, Batuka Bhairava, Siddh Jalpa, Siddh-Bhadra and Shiva Shambhu. His reign lasted for forty-one years, and he is said to have been hundred years old at the time of his death in 1727 CE. Two *ranis*, thirty *khwasis* and five maid servants burnt themselves on the funeral pyre as *sati*. It is also said that his son Shiv-Jawala Sen died in 1722 CE that is five years before his father. Shiv-Jawala Sen left two infant sons by separate *ranis*, who were born at the same time. To decide who should succeed, Sidh Sen placed a sword and pile of dust before them. One touched the sword and the other the dust, hence the names, *Shamsher*, 'sword'; *Dhurchatia*, 'dust eater'; from *dhul*-dust and *chatna* to taste. Shamsher Sen (1727 CE) was the son of Shiv-Jawala Sen and succeeded the *gaddi* at the age of five. The administration was run by Mian Jappu, an illegimate brother of Siddh Sen, during his minority. Soon after his accession a matrimonial alliance was arranged between Shamsher Sen and a daughter of Raja Ugar Singh of Chamba. In 1753, Bir belonging to Kullu was ravaged and occupied by Mandi forces. Raja Jai Singh of Kullu was driven out by the rival faction due to internal trouble and he sought refuge at Lahore. As such, Shamsher Sen took advantage of this turmoil and seized the Chuhar *ilaqa* along with the forts of Amargarh, Deogarh, Mastpur and Sari. In the fight between Mandi and Suket in the plains of Bahl just below Dodhe, Mandi was victorious after heavy loss of men and the Wazir of Suket was also killed. The later years of Shamsher Sen's reign were embittered by dissensions at home. Dhurchatia, his younger brother and minister had gradually acquired so much power that even the Raja was afraid of him. All the Mians or royal kinsmen were at his side, and it is even said that he proposed to set aside the heir-apparent–Surma Sen–or put him out of the way, so as to open the way to the *gaddi* for himself. The young prince, Surma Sen had to flee to Suket and Bilaspur and then to Nadaun, where an asylum was found at the Katoch Court with Raja Sansar Chand. After some time he returned with a force and expelled the Mians, Dhurchatia taking refuge in Suket. Raja Sansar Chand Katoch succeeded to the throne of Kangra after defeating the Sikh Chieftains in the plains in 1775 CE and claimed paramount authority over all the other states and compelled them to pay tribute and supply contingents for his military expeditions. Mandi had to acknowledge his supremacy and supply contingents for the invasion of Kullu. Shamsher Sen reigned for 54 years and died in 1781. He was succeeded by his son Surma Sen (1781 CE). All the Mians were powerless and the state prospered. Bairagi Ram, his Brahmin tutor, was his Wazir and ruled the state wisely. After short reign of seven years Surma Sen died in 1788, and as usual six *ranis,* six *khwasis* and four *rakhwalis* became *sati.* He was succeeded by his son Ishwari Sen (1788 CE), being a minor only five years old and the administration was retained in the hands of Bairagi Ram, the Wazir. In about 1792, Raja Sansar Chand invaded Mandi and plundered the capital. Raja Ishwari Sen of Mandi was detained as a prisoner at Sansar Chand's Court for twelve years and the state was left in the hands of its ministers and ordered to pay a tribute of one lakh of rupees. Deprived of the presence of their ruler and robbed of some of the richest provinces, Mandi continued to struggle against its hard lot. Kamlahgarh alone was saved from falling in to Sansar Chand's hands. With the defeat of Sansar Chand at the hand of the Gorkhas at Mahal Mori, Ishwari Sen of Mandi was liberated from his confinement. Ranjit Singh, in May 1809, advanced to the hills with a large army and a treaty having been concluded at Jwalamukhi, he compelled the Gorkhas to retire across the Satluj. Most of other hill states became tributary to Ranjit Singh and Mandi was made to pay an annual tribute of rupees thirty thousand and subsequently in years 1816-17, it was raised to one lakh. It was again reduced by judicious bribery to rupees fifty thousand. The districts alienated by Raja Sansar Chand were restored to the state. During the latter part of his reign, Mandi offered asylum to ex-Raja of Bashahr and Nagpur and made liberal provision for them. It was during his reign, in March, 1820, the first Europeans, namely, William Moorcroft and Trebeck visited Mandi en-route to Ladakh. Ishwari Sen was a religious minded person and he left no legitimate male heir and the state was passed on to his younger brother Zalam Sen whose past conduct did not augur well for the state. He died in 1826 CE and as many as 26 ladies of his harem became *sati* with him. Zalam Sen was cruel and capricious, and the administration of the state was given to his nephew, Balbir Sen, one of the younger sons of Ishwari Sen by a concubine. His oppressive methods in extorting money from his subjects have become proverbial. He had to pay a lakh of rupees as succession duty and tribute of rupees seventy thousand to Lahore. There is nothing worthy of record in the time of Zalam Sen. He left this world unwept, unhonoured and unsung in year 1839 CE with no legitimate male hair. Mian Balbir Sen, the third *sartora* of Raja Ishwari Sen was recognized as his successor which was resented by the Mians, and more especially by the descendants of Dhurchatia, the brother of Raja Shamsher Sen, who were in the legitimate line of descent. Balbir Sen was twenty-one years of age at the time of his accession; two months afterwards, Vigne visited Mandi. He mentioned about Raja Balbir Sen that :

> "The Rajah himself was short, stout in person, with a jovial, good-natured, and remarkably European-like countenance. He was uncommonly civil, and prodigal of his expressions of regard and friendship for the English, and, unlike many other Rajahs, he allowed me to depart when I wished, without pressing me to stay a day longer than suited my convenience."

In the year 1839 Maharaja Ranjit Singh occupied Mandi but he died on 27 June 1839. It was the beginning of disintegration of Sikh power in the hills and the British emerged as the most powerful. Balbir Sen's accession practically synchronized with the death of Maharaja Ranjit

Singh; and Kharak Singh, the only son was too weak in intellect to control the misrule and anarchy that his father's death had set in motion; and he and his dashing son were soon butchered in cold blood. Ranjit Singh had made his power felt in the hill states, and all the hill-chiefs owed him allegiance. At that time the conquest of Ladakh and Tibet was much talked about in Lahore, and before an expedition was dispatched, it was thought necessary to reduce Mandi completely, and especially not to leave in the rear the strong fortress of Kamlahgarh.

In June 1840, General Ventura, the leader of the French party at Lahore with a strong force was sent to Mandi and advanced to within seven miles of the state capital. From there General Ventura went to demand for payment of certain arrears of tribute, which was the ostensible excuse for the expedition. This demand was at once complied with. Balbir Sen wrote to Col. Tapp, Political Agent at Sabathu for an asylum for himself and his family in the British Territory which was agreed upon but expressed his inability to do any thing more for him. Mandi town was occupied and Balbir Sen, being helpless, agreed to every demand, and all the forts were surrendered. The Raja was sent as a prisoner to Amritsar and confined in the fort of Govindgarh. General Ventura then subdued the country and advanced to Kullu after which he returned to Lahore in December bearing the trophies of 200 forts. On his departure, Sikh force was left at Mandi under Col. Foulkes and the force mutinied. Before he could escape, he was cut down and was thrown into the funeral pyre while still alive.

In January, 1841 Sher Singh became the Maharaja of Lahore and on the following May, Balbir Sen was set at liberty and permitted to return to Mandi, taking with him the image of the goddess Devi, which had been carried away by the Sikhs from Kamlahgarh. Balbir Sen maintained a secret communication for protection by the British with Erskine, the Superintendent of Hill States. Immediately after the battle of Sobraon between the British and the Sikhs, Balbir Sen and the Raja of Suket sent a confidential agent named Sibu Pandit to Erskine tendering their allegiance to the British government; the two Chiefs visited him at Bilaspur.

On 9th March, 1846, a treaty was concluded between the British and the Sikh Darbar. The entire Doab, between the Satluj and the Beas including Mandi and Suket States came under the direct control of the British government and placed under the charge of the Commissioner of Jalandhar. In the autumn of 1846, John Lawrence, Commissioner of Jalandhar visited Mandi on his way to Kullu and advised the Raja to build roads in the state. Barnes, the first Deputy Commissioner of Kangra, also settled the boundaries between Mandi, Suket and Kangra. Raja Balbir Sen died on 26th January, 1851, leaving three sons, Bijai Sen, Pradhan Singh and Man Singh. Bijai Sen was only four years old. The entire state was plunged into mourning and the state had now come under British protection and the custom of *sati*, etc. was put down.

On the demise of the late Raja, mother of Raja Bijai Sen, Anoop Naini, better known as Sahibini Sahiba made an attempt to take the reign of administration and possession of treasury in her own hands. Wazir Gosaon was still in office and was the ablest and most capable man in the State. His services were found to be indispensable and the Board of Administration approved his name as President of Council of Regency with other members. Subsequently, he was given the entire control of the administration, judicial and financial for the benefit of the State.

In the year 1859, Bijai Sen married the grand daughter of the Raja of Datarpur, and soon afterwards a niece of the Raja of Guler. Bhup Singh, a descendant of Dhurchatia was given an allowance of Rs.1220 a year with the condition not to enter or disturb the Mandi state.

In the year 1863, Lord Elgin, the first Viceroy of India toured the hills and on his way from Kullu, he halted at Badhwani, Jhatingiri and Darang. The Raja with his mother went to Darang for an interview. In the year 1864, the Government granted the Raja a salute of 11 guns; and on 12th October 1866, having attained majority, he was formally invested by Sir Douglas Forsyth with the power of a ruling prince. On this occasion he donated one lakh of rupees for works of public utility in the state including a school, hospital, post-office in the town, mule road from Baijnath to Sultanpur in Kullu, over the Babu Pass, sarais and travellers' bunglows along the line of road from Kangra valley, through Mandi, towards Kullu and Shimla. The boundary between Mandi and Suket, on the Halti side was also finally settled by the Commissioner of Jalandhar.

In October 1871, Lord Mayo, the Viceroy of India along with A. Brandreth, Commissioner of Jalandhar, paid a visit to Mandi and a Darbar was held in the Bera in which all the State officials, Jagirdars and principal residents were present. During his reign the other government officials who visited Mandi state were: Lieutenant-Governor of Panjab, Sir Henry Davies in 1874 and Sir Robert Egerton in October 1880; Sir Charles Aitcheson with Col. Gordon Young, the Commissioner in 1883; Sir Dennis Fitzpatrick in 1894; and Sir W. Mackworth Young with A. Anderson, the Commissioner in November 1901. Iron suspension bridge over the Suketi nala, near Mandi was opened by Sir Dennis Fitzpatrick during his visit in 1894 and it was named "The Fitzpatrick Suspension Bridge".

In February 1870, Wazir Gosaon died and the administration was looked after by the Raja assisted by his brother Mian Pradhan Singh, who was very popular with the people. He, however, died in 1875 and Mian Uttam Singh was appointed Wazir in his place. In 1878, Mian Man Singh, the younger brother of the Raja was appointed to succeed him. But again Mian Uttam Singh was recalled to office at the end of 1880 and continued up to October 1888, when he died, and Jawahar Lal was appointed to succeed him.

In 1877, Raja Bijai Sen attended the Proclamation Darbar at Delhi, and, in commemoration of the event, he caused to be built the Victoria Suspension Bridge over the Beas at Mandi at an expense of one lakh rupees. The construction of new roads from Mandi to Kullu by Dulchi Pass with a suspension bridge over the Uhl river at the cost of rupees forty thousand, a cart road from Baijnath to Mandi and another one from Mandi to Bhamla was started by the state. In the year 1884, two daughters of Raja Bijai Sen were married to the heir apparent of Bashahar.

The period from 1894 to 1900 was unfortunate for the State and two sons of the Raja died in infancy. The Raja himself was not keeping well and Mian Uttam Singh and Fendall, the British officer did not work together. At last both of them were removed from the office and Padha Jiwanand was recalled from Jodhpur state, where he was a Member of the State Council, and appointed as Wazir. Improvement of administration was recogonized by the Government and he was bestowed the title of Rai Bahadur. Raja Bijai Sen died in 1902. In recognition of his general good government, it had been decided to invest him at the Delhi Darbar, on the accession of King Edward VII, with the title of K.C.S.I. and this was announced in the *Honours Gazette* three weeks after his death. Many public utility services and facilities like schools, hospitals and post offices, etc., had been started by Raja Bijai Sen during his time. He had also built large number of palaces and houses. A mule road from Baijnath in district Kangra to Sultanpur in the adjoining district of Kullu, via Mandi and the Victoria Suspension Bridge on the river Beas were constructed during his time in the year 1877.

He died on December, 1902 and left no direct heir and Kanwar Bhawani Sen, his illegitimate son, was recognized as his successor and was formally installed in November 1903 by Sir Charles Rivaz, Lieutenant-Governor of the Panjab as Raja of Mandi. The installation *darbar* was held in the open space in front of the Naya Mahal, but the Raj Tilak was performed in the Madho Rai temple in Damdama palace. Being a minor, Millar, ICS was appointed Superintendent of the State on 30 November 1903. Bhawani Sen completed his studies at the Chief's College in Lahore under the care of his tutor, E.M. Atkinson and returned to Mandi on the 17th April, 1904. The State sustained major loss due to earthquake of 4th April, 1905 and the total loss of life in the State was estimated to about 1500 and the damage to the property was enormous. At that time Raja and Mr Millar were in the Dak Bungalow at Palampur and had a narrow escape. The State acted with great liberty, grain loans were given from the stores, *takawi* loans to those who had suffered loss, timber to the value of more than one lakh of rupees was given to the homeless, free of charge.

On 7th October, 1905, the Raja was formally given full administrative powers and in November 1905, he visited Lahore with other Punjab chiefs to meet the Prince of Wales. In the year 1906, Darbar Hall was built at a cost of rupees fifty thousand and he ordered for construction of residence for him as Bhawani Niwas, which was completed after his death, besides carrying out repairs to the several neglected temples and buildings. Lord Kitchener passed through Mandi territory on his way from Shimla to Kangra and in 1908, Sir Louis Dane, Lieutenent-Governor of the Punjab, came from Kullu via Dulchi Pass and halted for a day in the Residency, on his way to install Mian Bhim Sen as the Raja of Suket.

In the beginning of 1909, serious agrarian disturbance alleging oppression at the hands of certain officials of the State broke out and the zamindars of the region proceeded to Mandi to present their grievances before the Raja. The revolt led by Shobha Ram against the repressive, corrupt and arrogant administration of Raja Bhawani Sen and his Wazir Jiwa Nand Padha was sorted out and the ring leaders were punished. Padha Jiwa Nand was dismissed and Inder Singh, the son of late Wazir Uttam Singh was appointed the Wazir. In December 1911, Raja Bhawani Sen also attended the Coronation Darbar at Delhi. Soon after his return he fell ill and died at the end of January 1912 at the age of twenty-nine without any male heir to succeed him.

On 10th April, 1913, Jogendra Sen, the son of late Mian Kishen Singh, the nearest male relative, was formally installed as the next Raja of Mandi State by Sir Louis Dane, Lieutenant-Governor of the Punjab. A.L. Gordon Walkar, ICS was appointed Superintendent of the State and in 1916 he was relieved by H.W. Emerson. With this, the post of Wazir was abolished and Munshi Amar Singh was appointed as Assistant Superintendant. Raja being a minor of eight years of age was admitted to the Queen Mary's College, Lahore, under the care of his tutor, T.P. Gillmore and remained there till 1923 for obtaining his Diploma. He then began his training in judicial, executive and revenue areas. In October 1916 he joined the Aitchison Chiefs College, Lahore. In February 1925, he was invested with full powers as a Ruling Chief by Col. A.B. Minchin, Agent to the Lieutenent-Governor of the Punjab States. H.J. Maynard, ICS, Commissioner and Superintendent of Jalandhar Division, visited Mandi in October 1914 after twenty-six years and inspected the State Courts and some of the State schools. He also held a public darbar on the relations between the Raja and his subjects. Rules were framed for social reforms so as to regulate marriage and death expenses. Fishing and shooting rules were introduced, road between Baijnath and Mandi was widened. Mandi Municipal Committee was created in 1910-11. The Anglo-Vernacular Middle School building at Mandi was raised to double storey at the cost of rupees ten thousand and seven new schools were opened in the rural areas. The devastating fire that broke out on the night of 10th January, 1916 destroyed and damaged almost all the records and files of the State Courts and offices. With the introduction of new settlement, the *begar* was abolished from 1st January 1917 and at the same time a system of payment was introduced for all casual *begar* except the very minor services rendered in connection with the camps of officials. In the same year in the month of April, the Raja alongwith other official staff attended the Viceregal Darbar at Lahore. On reaching the age of 19, proposal for his marriage were set afoot and he was married with Kumari Amrit Kaur, the only daughter of the Maharaja of Kapurthala on 5th February, 1923 and in December a son was born and *namkaran* ceremony was performed and named Yashodhan Singh. During the period of his minority, Mandi remained under the management of a British Officer and a number of departments were overhauled and reorganised. During 1922-23, the survey of Hydro-electric Project at Uhl valley was carried out and got sanctioned from Punjab Government with an agreement on 28th February, 1925. On 9th May, 1924, Raja Jogindra Sen in the company of other state officials visited Europe and on his return, he proceeded to Calcutta for military training. The State forces were reorganized and named after as His Highness Jogindra Infantry and the Jogindra Lancers. On 1st November 1921, both the state of Mandi and Suket were transferred from the political control of Punjab Government to that of Government of India till India's independence on 15th August 1947. On 8th March, 1948, Raja Jogindra Sen, the last Raja of Mandi, decided to abolished the separate symbol of Mandi State and finally became a part of newly-formed Himachal Pradesh on 15th April, 1948.

3
Monumental Remains of Mandi

The historicity and sacred character of Mandi, the 'Chhoti Kashi' or 'Kashi of the Hills' is well exemplified by a number of archaeological remains in the form of temples, rock-cut shrines, historical buildings and royal memorial stones (*barselas*) of the rulers and members of the ruling family of Mandi state. Most of the temples were built along the banks of the Suketi and Beas rivers and also within the town between the sixteenth and nineteenth centuries. These temples are mainly of stone and in Nagara as well as domical styles which comprises of *garbhagriha* surmounted by *sikhara,antarala*, *mandapa* and porch, usually decorated with carvings. Another feature is the trefoil arch which rests on the capital of the pillars or pilasters, and the brackets are often shaped as human figures, seated on the head of an elephant and holding the trunk in their hands. The corners are sometimes embellished by the figures of celestial musicians. Most of the temples are dedicated to Shiva and the goddess Shakti. Shiva is shown in several forms, the commonest being five-faced Shiva or the Panchavaktra or three-faced Shiva as Trilokinath or as Ardhanarishvara, the half body is of Shiva and the other half of Parvati. The goddess goes by several names. Siddh Shambhu temple is actually a monolithic rock-cut site representing a Shiva-*linga* in the centre of a *yonipatta* at the base, both fashioned as if resting upon a small platform, with Nandi seated at the base of the platform. The Devi temples in the town are Bhuvaneshvari Devi, Jalpa Mata temple, Shyama Kali temple, Sitala Mata temple, Siddh-Kali temple mostly dating from seventeenth century onwards. The important Vaishnava temples in the town are the Jagannatha temple, the image of which is said to have been brought to Mandi by Raja Gur Sen (1679-1684) from Odisha during his pilgrimage, other being Madho Rai and Ramachandra temples. Three temples namely, Parkash Dei, Rajrajeshvari Devi and Baba Kot are located within the Damdama Palace complex while Bhatanti Mahadeva temple is inside the Bhawani Palace; entry to these shrines is restricted for the general public. The other important historical buildings in the Mandi town are the Damdama Palace, Naya Mahal, Bhawani Palace, Raj Mahal, etc.The historical Gurudwara locally known as Gurudwara Palang Sahib was built in honour of Guru Gobind Singh, the 10th Sikh Guru, who spent some time in Mandi. The artistic and architectural features with their historical background of some of these have been briefly described and elaborated in the following pages:

(A) Shaiva Shrines

Bhutnatha Temple : The temple of Bhutnatha is located at a distance of about one km from the bus stand towards west within the congested and crowded locality of Bhutnatha Bazar. It was built by Raja Ajbar Sen in the year 1526 CE which marks the beginning of the establishment of new capital of the Mandi State. It is one of the most popular temples in Mandi town (Plates1-2; Fig.1 (a-d)). The temple facing east and is oriented east-west and stands amidst a spacious courtyard within an enclosure wall. It comprises of *garbhagriha* or sanctum sanctorum, *antarala*, a pillared *mandapa* and a porch.

Plate 1 : Bhutanatha Temple, Mandi

Plate 2 : Bhutanatha Temple, Mandi

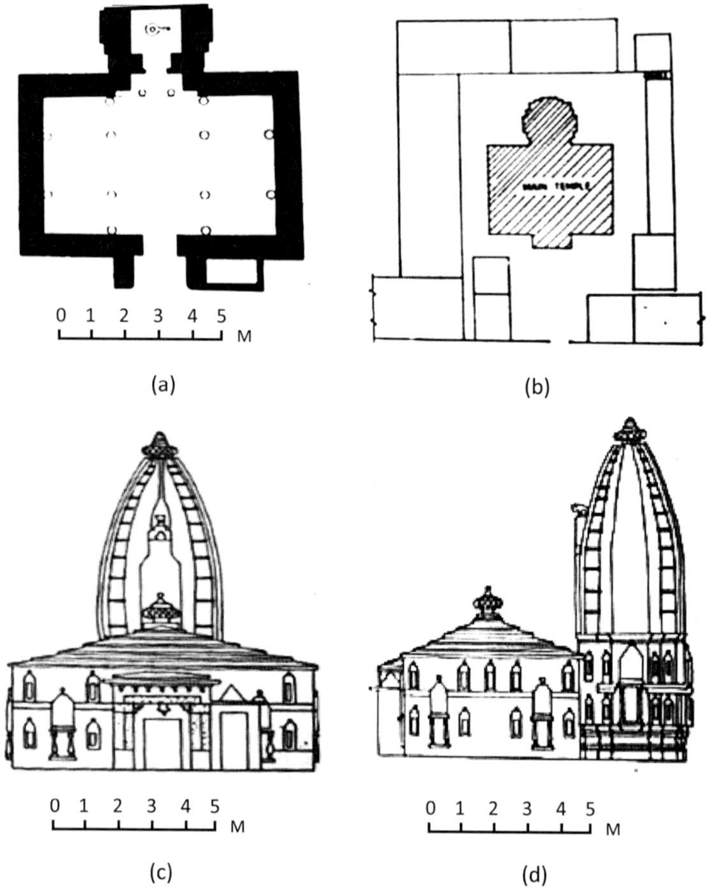

Fig. 1 (a-d) : Bhutnatha Temple, Mandi

The *garbhagriha* is square on plan and oriented east-west. Built of sandstone blocks, the elevation is in Nagara style consisting of *pitha, jangha, sikhara* and a finial capped by *amalaka* followed by a rectangular block topped by *kalasha* and *trisula*. Presently, it has been fully plastered with a thick lime plaster and oil painted. The ceiling is in receding tiers topped with lantern style roof. The façade is plain on sides while on the *lalatabimba* is the figure of Ganesha seated on *padma*. Above it and on the sides are different mouldings. The *garbhagriha* contains north facing Shiva-*linga.*The hooded snake is made of brass. The other figures in the sanctum are the image of Ganesha and six-armed Karttikeya in marble. On the exterior walls are shown figures of Brahma on the south and Bhairava towards north within the central *ratha* niches. The *antarala* is a small rectangular chamber oriented north-south with two pillars at its sides. It too has lantern type ceiling but is divided into two blocks. Its pillars have round torus with sixteen-sided shaft topped by *ghata-pallava* capital, abacus and a four sided bracket.

The façade is exquisitely carved with different motifs and carries a standing figure of Ganesha flanked by devotees on either side. The pillars are interlinked with arches carrying human and animal figures. The *mandapa* is a rectangular structure oriented north-south and facing east. It hosts ten pillars laid in a symmetrical form dividing it into nine blocks. Two podiums can also be seen towards north and south attached with the exterior wall portion. It is constructed in sandstone blocks and lime plastered and painted. The roof is in receding pyramidal style topped by a finial capped by *amalaka* and a *kalasha*. Its pillars have square torus topped with round shaft over which is a capital showing either *ghatapallava* motif or different deities followed by an abacus and a four-sided bracket. The nine blocks show lantern type ceiling with the central one having receding tiers. It contains *yajna-kund* and its *vibhuti* is put on the forehead with great reverence by the devotees. The porch is a simple rectangular structure devoid of any decoration. In front of the temple is the standing figure of Nandi over a platform. On the right of the main entrance is another shrine dedicated to Radha-Krishna built by one Vallabha and on the east is Satyanarayana temple built by one Jaysimha.

TrilokinathaTemple: Located on the right bank of the river Beas at Purani Mandi and dedicated to Shiva, this beautiful temple was built by Rani Sultana Devi, the wife of Raja Ajbar Sen in 1520 CE as per the inscription in Takri characters. Facing north-east, the temple is in *sikhara* style and comprises a square *garbhagriha*, an *antarala* and a spacious *mandapa* (Plates 3-6). A life-sized, three-faced stone image of Shiva with Parvati on the lap adorns the sanctum. The exterior wall of the sanctum showing a *pancharatha* plan is decorated with two rows of niches with the images of Uma-Maheshvara, Mahishasuramardini, and dancing figures. The *antarala* is surmounted by a *sukanasika* topped by a *bhadramukha.* The image of Ganesha is shown on the *lalatabimba* of the *antarala* which rests on the carved fluted columns showing a trefoiled *torana* springing from heads of two elephant riders in between them. Above is frieze showing musicians and dancers. Shaiva *dvarapala* carved on the sides guard the sanctum. The profusely carved door-frame of the sanctum has *shakhas* decorated with human figures and floral scrolls. The *mandapa* is rectangular on plan with miniature *sikharas* resting on elephant friezes in the four corners. Small niches decorate its exterior walls while two projecting balconies show horse riders and erotic scenes on the lateral sides. The slanting roof of the *mandapa* rests on four pillars. There is a large sculpture of Nandi placed on a raised pedestal in the centre of the *mandapa.* Loose sculptures are kept inside the *mandapa* and a few are stacked outside the temple. In addition to the main temple, there are other smaller and miniature temples, which are also dedicated to Shiva, and a small stepped pond, being the source of spring water for ablution.

Plate 3 : Trilokinatha Temple, Mandi

Plate 4 : Trilokinatha Temple, Mandi

Plate 5 : Trilokinatha Temple, Mandi

Plates 6 : Trilokinatha Temple, Mandi

Panchavaktra Temple: Panchavaktra Temple is located in Paddal Mohalla of Mandi town on the left side of the river Beas at the confluence of the Beas and Suketi Nala (Khad). It is one of the most important monuments in Mandi and is dedicated to Shiva, who is worshipped here in five forms, designated by five faces, hence the name, Panchavaktra. It is said that there were heavy rains in the year 1717 and the Beas and Suketi rivers were flooded to such an extent that the temple was completely submerged and the remaining few shrines were swept away. It was therefore built on a raised platform so that the flood water does not enter the temple premises. Facing north-east, the temple is in Nagara style with a sanctum, vestibule (*antarala*) and a pillared hall (*mandapa*) on plan (Fig.2 (a-c) Plates 7-8).

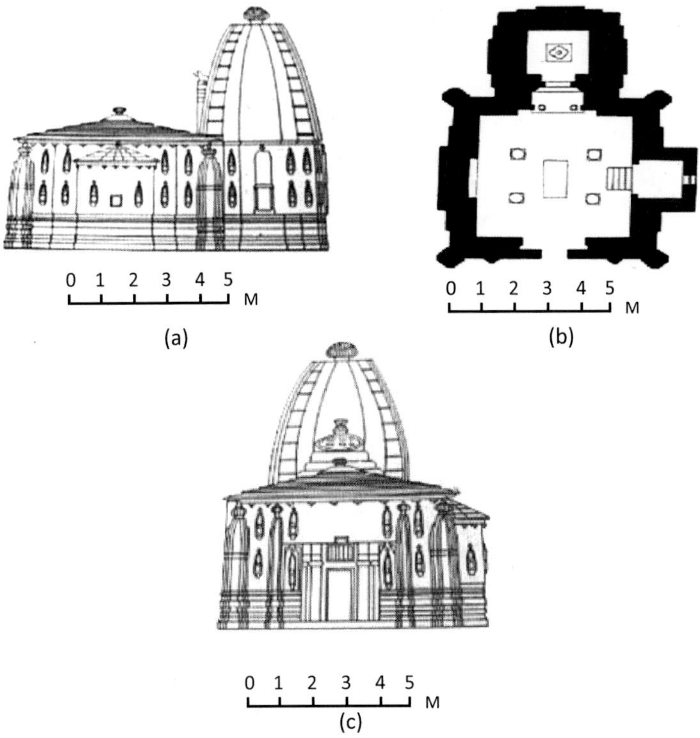

Fig.2 (a-c) : Panchavaktra Temple, Mandi

Plate 7 : Panchavaktra Temple, Mandi

Plate 8 : Panchavaktra Temple, Mandi

The sanctum of the temple is crowned by a curvilinear *sikhara* showing five rathas decorated with miniature *chaitya* window motifs while the corners above the *jangha* have *bhumiamalakas*. A five-faced Shiva, four on the sides and the fifth facing upwards and Parvati on the lap adorns the sanctum. These five forms (faces of Shiva) worshipped are Aghora, Ishana, Sadyojata, Vamadeva, and Tatpurusha. The image has ten arms. The exuberantly carved front of the *antarala* shows dancing figures and floral designs and the roof rests on two carved fluted stone columns. The *mandapa* is supported on four huge circular stone columns, the capitals of which are carved with floral bands and *ghatapallava* motifs. The *mandapa* on its outer corners is recessed with miniature shrines and its walls are decorated with two rows of niches displaying the images of deities and dancers. An image of Nandi is placed on a stone pedestal in the centre of the *mandapa*.The temple is traditionally associated with Raja Ajbar Sen; however scholars attributed the date of its construction to Raja Sidh Sen (1684-1727). It is evident that the present temple was re-built in place of the old structure, which was damaged by flood in the early nineteenth century.

Within the Panchavaktra temple complex is the temple, locally known as Batuk Bhairava temple which is under worship. Facing north-east, the temple with a *garbhagriha* super-imposed by a *sikhara* is so named as it houses an image of Batuk Bhairava in its *garbhagriha*. The temple can be placed in the second phase of temple architecture in Mandi. The temple stands on a low platform (*jagati*), has a distylar portal preceding the entrance and an elongated lofty *sikhara* over the *garbhagriha*. Representing classical temple architectural norms of the contemporary period, the temple of Batuk Bhairava has been protected alongside the Panchvaktra temple by Archaeological Survey of India and declared in 1952 as a monument of national importance.

Ardhanarishvara Temple: Among the temples in Mandi, the Ardhanarishvara temple is one of finest from aesthetic as well as architectural stand-point; unfortunately, the roof of the *mandapa* is incomplete (Plate 9). Located in the heart of the city across the river Beas, the Ardhanarishvara temple consists on plan a *pancharatha* sanctum, a *mandapa* and an *antarala* laid on a single north-south axis (Fig.3 (a-b)). The sanctum is almost square internally, in the centre of which is enshrined a small *linga* in grey sandstone fixed on a simple *yoni-pitha.* Behind it is a loose image of Ardhanarishvara in which Shiva is portrayed with knotted hair, wearing garland of human skulls, a serpent, with a musical instrument in one hand and a *damaru* in the other, while Parvati is shown wearing a diadem, an ear-ring and a nose-ring, the *vahana* of which is a four-legged composite animal having heads of bull and tiger.

Plate 9 : Ardhanarishvara Temple, Mandi

The image has four-arms the right hands holds *pasha* and *damaru* while in the left hands with bangles is holding *akshamala* in the upper left and a round object. The third eye is shown on the forehead. The image is shown wearing *karanda-mukuta* and half moon is quite prominent on the forehead. On the right and left respectively are images of Bhairava and Hanumana.The other images in the sanctum include badly-weathered Uma-Mahesvara and Ganesha in

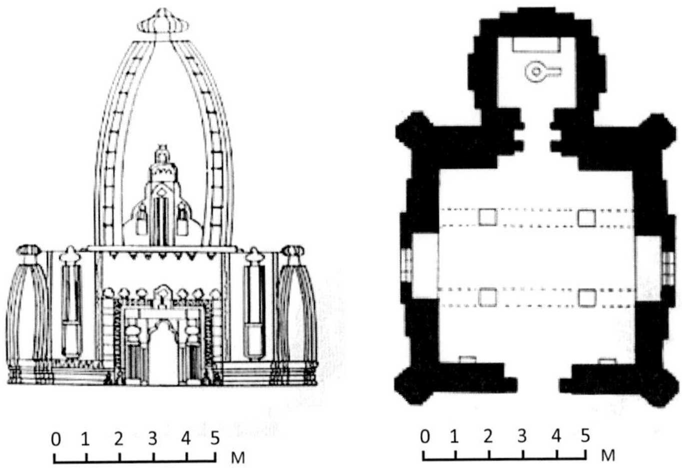

(a) (b)

Fig.3 (a-b) : Ardhanarishvara temple, Mandi

red sandstone. The *antarala*, locally known by the name *'dehri'* or *'dehli'* is very small as compared to the *mandapa* and the sanctum. Four pillars, two on each side, support the roof of the *antarala*. The facing two pillars are decorated with *mithuna* figures and *vidyadharas*. In the space between two pillars on each side, images of Hanumana and Shiva-*gana* in grey sandstone are placed; these were evidently placed at a later date. The image of Ganesha is carved in the centre of the *lalatabimba.* Foliated patterns decorate the door-jamb as well as the lintel over the gate of the sanctum. The *mandapa* is rectangular in plan with four *sikhara* in the four corners. The horizontal roof, now missing, is supported on four pillars. The pillars have a square base with design of embossed lotus and a circular shaft. The capital of the pillars is decorated with *ghata-pallava* pattern. Two rectangular windows open on the west and the east of the *mandapa.* The bordering slabs of the windows have diamond pattern which is a feature of the medieval temples. The entrance to the *mandapa* has a pilaster on each side. The flanking door-jambs contain figures of *dvarapalas* holding *nidhi*. The lintel is divided into two bands in which standing figures of Shiva and Parvati are carved in the centre of the upper band while the image of seated Ganesha is carved in the centre of the lower band. The other sculptures in the *mandapa* are: four-armed standing image of Brahma holding gourd, standing pot-bellied *dvarapala* and standing Mundamaleshvara wearing garland of skulls and lion cloth, bald headed, all in grey sandstone. On elevation, the temple comprises of *jagati, adhisthana, jangha, sikhara, griva* and *amalaka*. The *jagati* or the platform, built of dressed grey sandstone, is simple and undecorated and has a *ghata-pallava* or leaf pattern at intervals. The *adhishthana* portion has three offsets alternating with recessed bands. The offsets are decorated with honey suckle, leaf and geometrical designs. The lowest recessed band, which is the largest, has the figures of elephant and duck with a plant in-between. The *jangha* of the wall portion comprises of two superimposed bands of subsidiary *sikharas* on the wall of the *mandapa* as well as the sanctum. The niches in the miniature *sikharas* of the *mandapa* contain figures of *apsarases, vidyadharas* and *mithuna* figures. The adjoining bands of the *jangha* are decorated with leaf, diamond and faunal patterns. The main niches on the *jangha* of the sanctum contain images of Karttikeya and Kubera; the third, facing south, is without any image. On the recessed bands *vidyadharas* and *ganas* are represented. The *sikhara* is curvilinear having angular corners. On the front is a subsidiary *sikhara* over which is the *kirttimukha* topped by a *vyala* figure. Small miniature shrines are built into the *sikhara*, imparting it the appearance of ascending order. The *griva* is short and recessed and is capped by two receding *amalakas*. The *kalasha* portion is completely lost.

Shiva-Deula (Bijali-Mahadeva) temple: Dedicated to Mahadeva, this temple is located in lower Samkhetar area of Mandi town and situated south of Hanuman Ghat and Ekadasharudra temple. Built in domical style, it is rectangular on plan, facing north and oriented north-south. It comprises of a *garbhagriha*, an *antarala*, porch, Nandi platform, an enclosure wall with an entrance gateway (Fig.4 (a-c); Plates 10-11). The *garbhagriha* is square and facing north with elevation showing the platform topped by *pitha* with *khura, kumbha* and *kapota* mouldings followed by a *jangha* supporting the domical style roof over which is the finial marked by a base, an *amalaka*, two *kalashas*, a cone and a *dhvaja-stambha.*

The *garbhagriha* has a Shiva-*linga* at the centre while a figure of Ganesha and two other unidentified deities are attached to the western wall. Internally, it is devoid of any decoration. The flooring is of marble while the ceiling is in domical style. Externally, the platform is plain and devoid of any decoration while the *pitha* shows *khura*, *kumbha* and *kapota* mouldings. The *jangha* has a single miniature

Plate 10 : Shiva-Deula (Bijali-Mahadeva) Temple, Mandi

Plate 11 : Shiva-Deula (Bijali-Mahadeva) Temple, Mandi

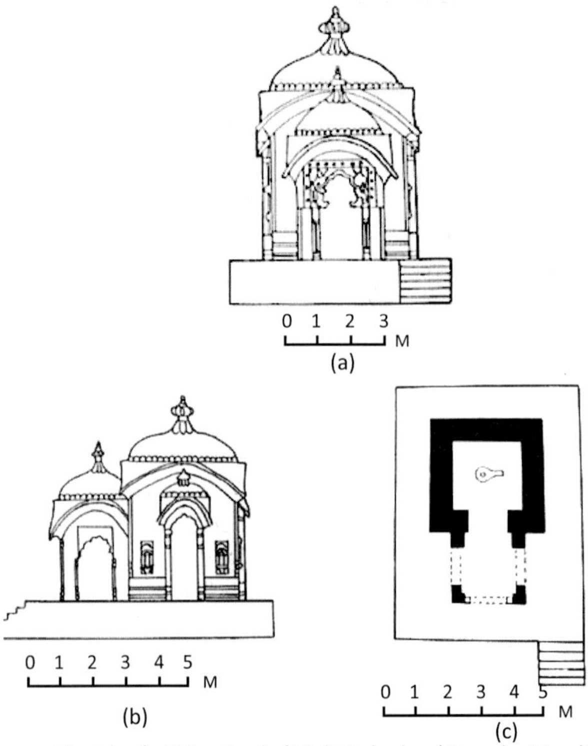

Fig. 4 (a-c) : Shiva-Deula (Bijali Mahadeva) Temple, Mandi

sikhara like niche on either side topped by a niche in low relief. The central *bhadrapaga* of both *pitha* and *jangha* has two pilasters with rectangular niche inside is low relief. The pilasters are topped by cusped arch followed by plain arch, a dome and a finial, all in low relief. The dome of the *sikhara* shows figure of a seated deity towards east. The base and top of the dome are decorated with lotus designs. The *antarala* is rectangular on plan facing north and is entered through a four-tiered door-jamb decorated respectively by floral scroll, lotus petals, fish-scales and zig-zag motifs. At the base of the four-tiered door-jamb is a *dvarapala* figure on either side while Ganesha is shown seated in the *lalatabimba.* The flooring is of marble while the ceiling is plain and flat. Externally, it shows the *pitha* and *jangha* mouldings similar to those in the *garbhagriha.* Followed by *antarala* is a square open porch facing north, oriented north-south with elevation showing the platform topped by pilasters on the back wall and pillars on the front interlinked with cusped arches supporting the domical *sikhara* topped by a finial, an *amalaka*, two *kalashas* and a *bijapuraka*.

Its façade shows two pillars topped by elephant riders followed by cusped arch carrying two musicians one each on either side. The door-jamb alongwith musicians show floral designs while a *bhadramukha* is shown on the *lalatabimba.* The pillars show small low relief pilasters decorated with floral designs. Flooring is of marble while the ceiling is in conical style. Along the enclosure wall is the entrance gate towards north with elevation showing pilasters on either side supporting first the cusped arch followed by plain arch over which is the domical *sikhara* with finial marked by a *bijapuraka.* The lotus moulding of the pilasters show elephant head jutting out while on the *lalatabimba* is the seated figure of Ganesha. The whole structure is built of dressed sandstone blocks plastered and coated with lime, both internally and externally.

Ekadasharudra Temple: The Ekadasharudra temple is located along the Hanuman Ghat, on the left bank of the Beas river, to the east of the Ramlingeshvara temple. The temple is approached from the courtyard through a small flight of steps. Built in typical *sikhara* style, it is *triratha* on plan and facing north, oriented north-south. It comprises of a *garbhagriha*, an *antarala*, a *mandapa*, a porch, an entrance gate (Fig.5 (a-c); Plates 12-13). The temple is provided with four corner shrines, dedicated to Suryanarayana, Tripurasundari and others. The *garbhagriha* is square, facing north with elevation showing the platform over which is the *pitha* and *jangha* supporting the curvilinear *sikhara* topped by a finial of an *amalaka*, three *kalasha*s, a vase and a *bijapuraka*.

Plate 12 : Ekadasharudra Temple, Mandi

Plate 13 : Ekadasharudra Temple, Mandi

(a)

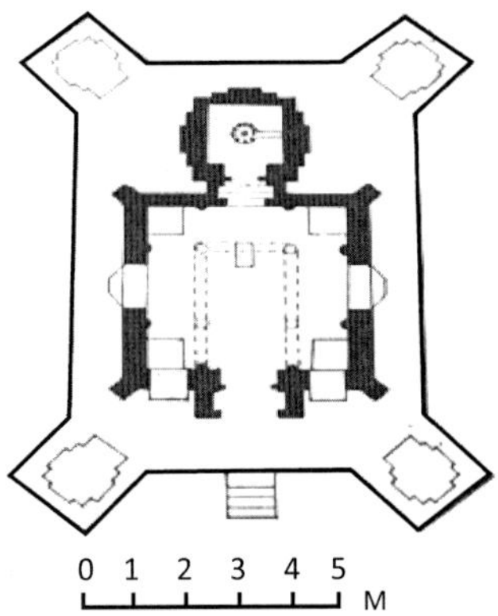

(b)

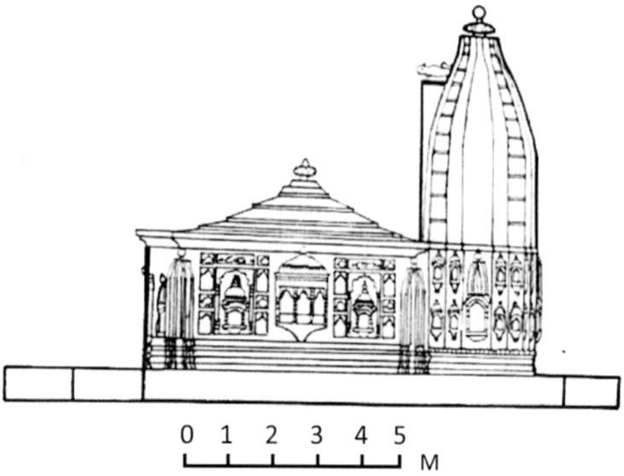

(b)

Fig. 5 (a-c) : Ekadasharudra Temple, Mandi

The *garbhagriha* is entered through a door-jamb with *dvarapala* figure on either side topped by three tiers of fish scales, lotus petals and spiral motif. Seated Ganesha is shown in the *lalatabimba*. Lintel is plain and undecorated. The *garbhagriha* within has in the centre marble Shiva-*linga* facing west and a figure of Ganesha. Back wall has been painted recently with figure of Shiva seated in *padmasana*. The flooring is of marble while the ceiling is of lantern style with central lotus medallion. Walls are devoid of any decoration except for an alcove on west. Externally, the *garbhagriha pranala* has of lion's face towards west. The *pitha* shows *khura, kumbha* and *kapota* mouldings while the *jangha* is divided into lower and upper parts. The central *bhadra paga* has niches, each flanked by four other niches on either side with two on lower *jangha* and two on upper *jangha*. The *bhadra* niche is decorated with inverted lotus designs. *Sikhara* has *amalaka* mouldings at corners and three projected stones on *bhadra-paga* each carrying figures of lions.

The *antarala* is rectangular on plan facing north, oriented east-west with two pillars at its front. Its elevation shows the platform over which is the *pitha* and *jangha* supporting the *sukanasika* topped by a *bhadra-mukha* and tiger figure. It can be entered through the pillars at sides over which are the elephant riders followed by cusped arch within which are the musician figures. Internally, it is devoid of any decoration. The flooring is of stone while the ceiling is flat. Externally, the *antarala* is devoid of any decoration.

In front of the *antarala* is a square four-pillared *mandapa* facing north with other eight-pilasters–two each on either wall. Its elevation shows the platform over which is the *pitha* and *jangha* supporting the flat receding pyramidal roof with over extending eaves and a finial marked by *amalaka, kalasha* and *bijapuraka.* The *mandapa* can be entered through a door-jamb with *dvarapala* figure on either side topped by three-tiered frame of fish-scales, lotus petals and spiral motifs. The *lalatabimba* shows figure of a seated Ganesha. Internally, the *mandapa* is devoid of any decoration. However, a Nandi is seen standing at the centre. There are stone podiums at all the four corners. The flooring is of stones while the ceiling is of nine unequal blocks in lantern style each topped by lotus medallion.

Externally, the platform is plain while the *pitha* with *khura*, *kapota* and lotus mouldings show floral and human pattern. The *jangha* shows projected window opening on the east and west and four *urushringas* at four corners. The window openings are flanked by a niche on either side. The western wall carries figures of Varaha and Kachhapa *avatara* of Vishnu on left and right respectively. The eastern wall carries figures of Narasimha and Vamanavatara on left and right respectively. Flanking these niches are again low-relief recesses with floral pattern at centre. These recesses are devoid of any figures. The southern wall shows figure of Matsyavatara towards west and Parashurama towards east. On the front wall i.e. the northern wall again there are two open projected window openings–one each on either side. The eaves are plain.

In front of the *mandapa* is a rectangular porch facing north, oriented east-west with two pillars at sides. Its elevation shows the platform over which is the *pitha* and *jangha* with over extending eaves supporting the flat superstructure. Its façade shows flying *gandharvas* in relief at sides topped by two-tiered floral door-jamb and three-tiered floral lintel. Pillars inside are topped by elephant riders over which is the cusped arch with figures of musicians in the centre. Internally it shows figure of *dvarapala* on either side over the walls. Flooring is of stone while ceiling is in domical shape with lotus medallion at the centre.

Externally, the corners show pilasters while the central portion has a figure of Lakshmi and Mahalakshmi on the western and eastern wall respectively. The four other shrines at the four corners are that of Surya-Narayana on the north-east, Vishnu in the north-west, Hanumana in the south-east and Durga/Shakti in the south-west. These are *dvi-ratha* on plan facing the main temple and comprising of a *garbhagriha* and a porch. The *garbhagriha* is square with elevation showing the platform over which is the *pitha* and *jangha* supporting the curvilinear *sikhara* and a finial marked by a base and *amalaka*. It can be entered through a plain façade wherein the deity is placed. Internally, it is devoid of any decoration while externally the *pitha* has *khura*, *kumbha* and lotus mouldings while the *jangha* is plain with a niche in the form of a *sikhara* at all three *bhadrapaga.* The *sikhara* is decorated with *amalaka* at corners. Followed by the *garbhagriha* is the open porch, rectangular on plan with two pillars at front and two pilasters at back. It too is devoid of any decoration.

The entire complex is enclosed by a wall with rectangular gateway towards north. This gateway facing north, oriented east-west shows in its elevation the walls with pilasters at corners supporting the flat roof. It has a beautiful door-jamb with five vertical niches on either side of which the lower ones have a *dvarapala* figure while upper four show figures of Hanumana, Vishnu, Brahma and Kuber on left and figures of Hanumana and Brahma on right respectively. The figure on *lalatabimba* shows a seated Ganesha. The whole complex is built of dressed sandstone blocks mortared with clay and plastered externally with cement and coated with oil paint. Apart from the above just below the temple, there are few stone sculptures kept inside miniature shrines and a huge Shiva-*linga* and Nandi is found carved on a rock facing the Beas river front (Plates 14-15).

Plate 14 : Stone Sculptures and rock-cut Siva-lingas

Plate 15 : Stone Sculptures and rock-cut Siva-lingas

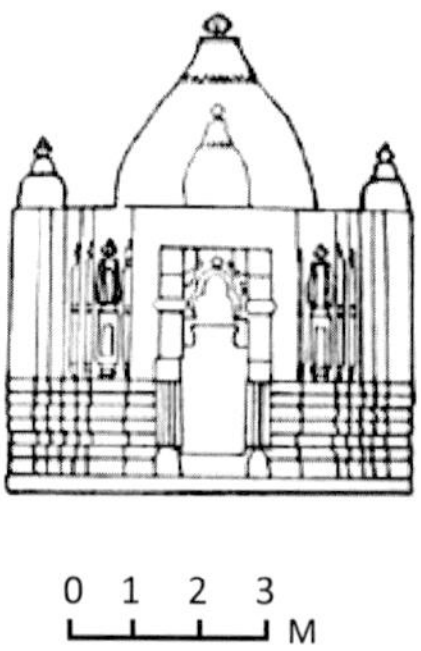

(a)

(b)

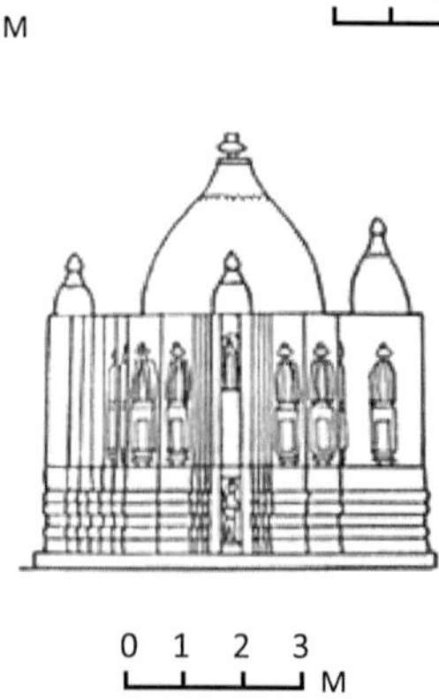

(c)

Fig. 6 (a-c) : Siddh-Bhadra Temple, Mandi

Siddh-Bhadra Temple: The temple of Siddh-Bhadra is located about 50 m east of Panchavaktra temple on the left bank of the Beas river. Built in typical *sikhara* style, it is *triratha* on plan facing north and oriented north-south comprising of the main *garbhagriha*, an *antarala*, a porch and followed by three other *garbhagrihas* on east, west and south. The temple stands on a very high rocky surface over a platform (Fig. 6(a-c); Plates 16-17).

Plate 16 : Siddh Bhadra Temple, Mandi

The main *garbhagriha* is square facing north with elevation showing the platform over which is the *pitha* and *jangha* supporting the domical *sikhara* and finial marked with an *amalaka*. The *garbhagriha* has an unidentified figure at the centre. Internally, it is decorated by a frieze of floral and human motif at the junction of *jangha* and *sikhara*. The flooring is of tiles while the ceiling is in

Plate 17 : Siddh Bhadra Temple, Mandi

domical shape. Externally, the platform is modern and devoid of any decoration. The *pitha* shows *khura* and *kumbha* motifs decorated with *padma* and *chaitya* motifs at intervals. The *jangha* shows various mouldings like floral scroll, inverted bell motif, fish-scals, floral, floral shell and floral scroll respectively from top to bottom. The niches can also be seen on either side. The *sikhara* is plain and devoid of any decoration. The *antarala* is rectangular in plan facing north, oriented east-west with elevation showing all the components of the main *garbhagriha*. However, there is no *sikhara* and the roof is flat. It is entered through a façade showing a *dvarapala* at the base on either side followed by a four-tiered door-jamb that is decorated by lotus petals, floral scroll, floral scroll and beads respectively. The *lalatabimba* shows seated Ganesha figure. Over the *lalatabimba* is the lintel with different horizontal tiers; the first tier or the lowest tier is ornamented by twelve lotus medallions within niches, followed upwards by the second having floral scroll, the third has twelve *kirtimukha* figures and the topmost one by floral motif. Internally, it is devoid of any decoration. Flooring is of tiles while the ceiling is flat and plain.

Externally, all the different mouldings of *pitha* and *jangha* are devoid of any decoration. In front of the *antarala* is the rectangular porch facing north, oriented east-west with two pillars. The elevation of the porch shows the same pattern like the main *garbhagriha.* The pillars on the sides are capped by elephant riders followed by cusped arches and musicians. The *lalatabimba* has a seated figure of Ganesha. The lintel on the top of all shows the first horizontal row of floral scroll followed by that of dancers and musicians. Internally, it is devoid of any decoration. Flooring is of tiles while the ceiling is flat. Externally, on the *jangha* portion there is a niche on either side with the figure of an attendant inside. Figure of a tiger can be seen in front of the porch facing the temple. The other three *garbhagrihas* present on the exterior of the main *garbhagriha* are rectangular on plan facing east, west and south respectively with elevation showing the platform over which are the *pitha* and *jangha* supporting the domical *sikhara* topped by a finial of *amalaka.* All the mouldings of *pitha* and *jangha* are externally like the main *garbhagriha.* The façade shows a figure of seated Ganesha in the lintel with panel showing series of diamond motif. It is topped by a bas-reliefs moulding like miniature *sikhara.* The niches on sides carry figures of musicians while the *sikhara* shows lotus figure on top and bottom of the dome. These three *garbhagrihas* have figures of Lakulisha on east, Hanuman on south and Siva on west. Internally, they are plain and devoid of any decoration. Besides there are other loose sculptures within the complex namely that of a seated four-handed Ganesha on the west of tiger at front, Gauri-Shankar and others towards eastern side and *Barsela* stones towards east of the façade of the porch. The whole temple is built of dressed sandstone.

Shiva-Rudra Temple: The temple of Shiva-Rudra is located in Bangla Mohalla near Suketi Khad. Built in domical style, it is rectangular on plan facing east and oriented east-west and comprising of a *garbhagriha*, an *antarala*, a porch, a Nandi figure and a gate (Fig.7 (a-c); Plate 18). The *garbhagriha* is square facing east and oriented east-west with elevation showing the platform topped by *pitha* and *jangha* supporting the domical *sikhara* over which is the finial marked by *kalasha*, *bijapuraka* and a trident. The *garbhagriha* has a Shiva-*linga* facing *ratha* at the centre while the walls show at their base figures of Ganesha and Durga on the north, Vishnu on the west and Surya on the south wall. Externally, the platform is plain and devoid of any decoration while the *pitha* shows *khura*, *kumbha* and *padma* mouldings. The *jangha* shows the central big *bhadra* niche flanked by two other on either side followed by pilasters at corners. The southern wall on *jangha* shows figure of Varaha in the centre flanked by Matsya and Kurma on the left and right. The western wall shows Parashurama in the centre flanked by Narasimha and an unidentified deity on either side.

The northern wall shows Vishnu on the Garuda in the centre flanked by Rama and Kalki (seated on bull and holding a sword and javelin) at its left right respectively. The arched portion shows at the centre lattice design. The *sikhara* has lotus design at the base and top. The *antarala* is rectangular on plan facing east and oriented north-south and is entered through a four-tiered door-jamb is a *dvarapala* figure on either side while Ganesha is shown seated in a niche on the *lalatabimba*. Internally, it is devoid of any decoration.

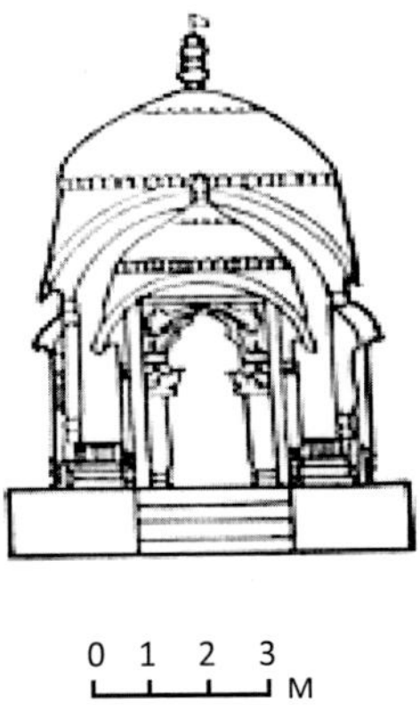

(a)

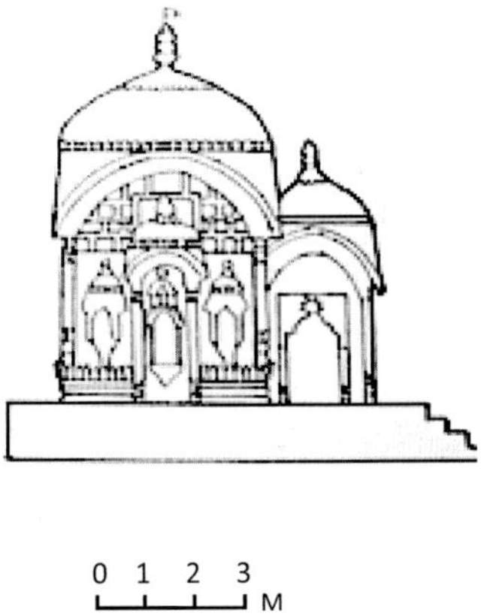

(b)

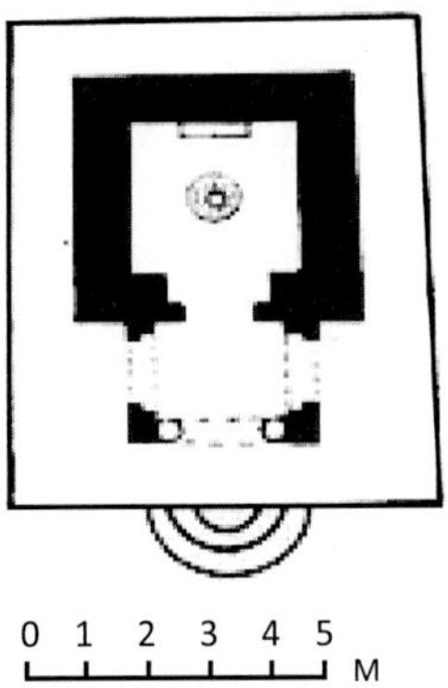

(c)

Fig. 7 (a-c) : Siva-Rudra Temple, Mandi

Externally, it is like the walls of the *garbhagriha* but shows a figure of Buddha within the niche towards east. *Sikhara* has a figure of a standing tiger facing east. It is followed by *antarala* and a square, open porch facing east, oriented east-west with elevation showing the platform topped by pilasters on the back wall and pillars on the front interlinked with cusped arch supporting the domical *sikhara* topped by finial of *amalaka*, *kalasha* and *bijapuraka*. Its façade shows two pillars topped by elephant riders followed by cusped arch carrying two musicians, one each on either side. The pillars show small pilasters in low relief decorated with floral designs especially lotus.

Plate 18 : Siva-Rudra Temple, Mandi

Flooring is of tiles while the ceiling shows receding rectangular stone slabs topped by lotus medallions. Externally, the pilasters are decorated with floral designs. Figure of Karttikeya is seen on the north and south. The domical *sikhara* has lotus design on its base and top. A standing figure of Nandi over a platform is seen outside the porch facing the temple. An entrance gateway is seen towards east along the oblong shaped enclosure wall. Its elevation shows the plain walls topped by domical roof and finial of a *bijapuraka*. Figures of Ganesha and Hanumana can be seen on the right and left respectively. The whole structure is built of dressed sandstone blocks. Internally, it has been renewed with tile work while externally, it is oil painted.

Mahadeva Temple: The temple of Mahadeva is located in Purani Mandi to the south of Sitala Mata temple. Built in domical style, it is square on plan facing north-east, oriented north-east-south-west and comprises of a *garbhagriha*, an *antarala* and an open porch (Fig.8 (a-c); Plate 19).

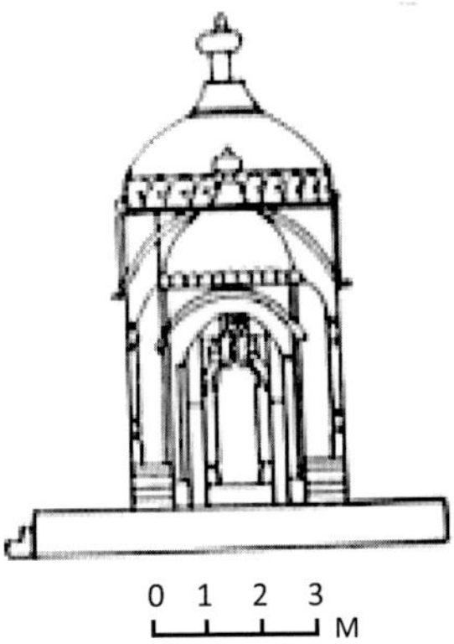

(a)

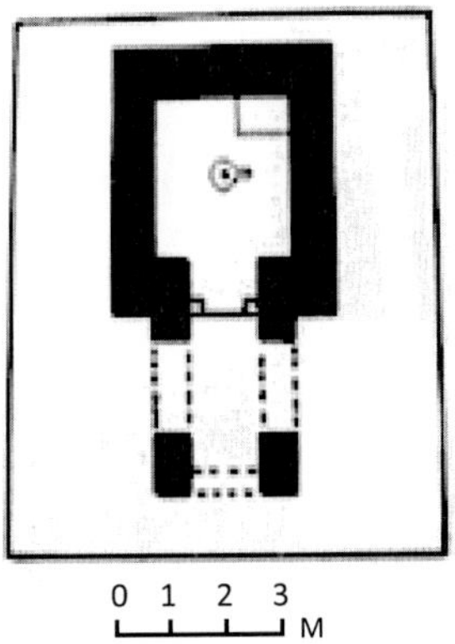

(b)

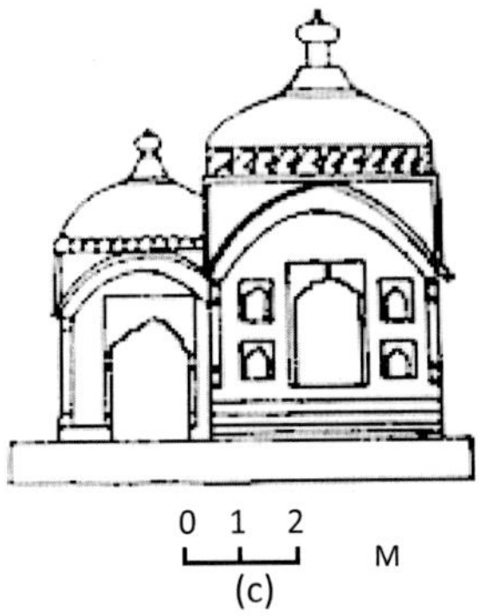

(c)

Fig. 8 (a-c) : Mahadeva Temple, Mandi

Plate 19 : Mahadeva Temple, Mandi

The *garbhagriha* is square facing north-east with elevation showing the plain platform topped by *pitha* with *khura* and *kumbha* mouldings followed by a *jangha* supporting the domical *sikhara* over which is the finial marked by a base, an *amalaka*, *bijapuraka* and a *dhvaja-stambha.*

In the *garbhagriha* is placed a Shiva-*linga* facing west at the centre while a figure of Radha Krishna in marble is kept on the platform towards south-west. Internally, it is devoid of any decoration except for a niche at the centre of each wall white-washed with lime. The southern niche shows four-handed Lakshmi seated in *padmasana* over lotus platform with upper right and left holding a lotus each and lower right and lower left holding a *pharsa* and a *pasa* respectively. She is shown ornamented and wears a crown over the head. The deity on the eastern niche is the six-headed, four-armed Karttikeya seated on peacock holding a snake in its beak shown over a pedestal. The deity on the western niche is seated Ganesha while on the north-western corner is placed a four-handed figure of Durga seated on tiger holding a sword in upper right hand, an arrow in lower right, a shield in upper left and bow in lower left and topped by an umbrella. The flooring is of marble while the ceiling is in conical shape with octagonal base.

Externally, the platform is plain and devoid of any decoration while the *pitha* shows *khura* and *kumbha* mouldings. The *jangha* and the *sikhara* show lotus and vase-and-foliage motifs on various parts. The *jangha* also has a big niche at the centre flanked by two other niches on low relief on its either side and followed by pilasters at the corners. The *antarala* is rectangular on plan facing north-east and is entered through a three-tiered door-jamb decorated with floral scroll, lotus petals and scroll from inside to outside and rests on a male *dvarapala* figure on either side while the *lalatabimba* shows a four-armed seated Ganesha. Externally, it is merged between *garbhagriha* and porch. In front of *antarala* is a square open porch facing north-east, oriented northeast-southwest with elevation showing the platform topped by pilasters on the back wall and pillars on the front interlinked with cusped arches supporting the domical *sikhara* topped by finial of base, an *antarala*, *bijapuraka* and a *dhvajastambha*. Its façade shows two pillars interlinked with cusped arches and carrying two musicians, one each on either side topped by three-headed *bhadra-mukha.*

Inside is a stone figure of seated Nandi over pedestal facing south. Flooring is of marble while the ceiling shows receding rectangles, externally it is plain. The whole structure is built of dressed sandstone blocks plastered with cement and whitewashed.

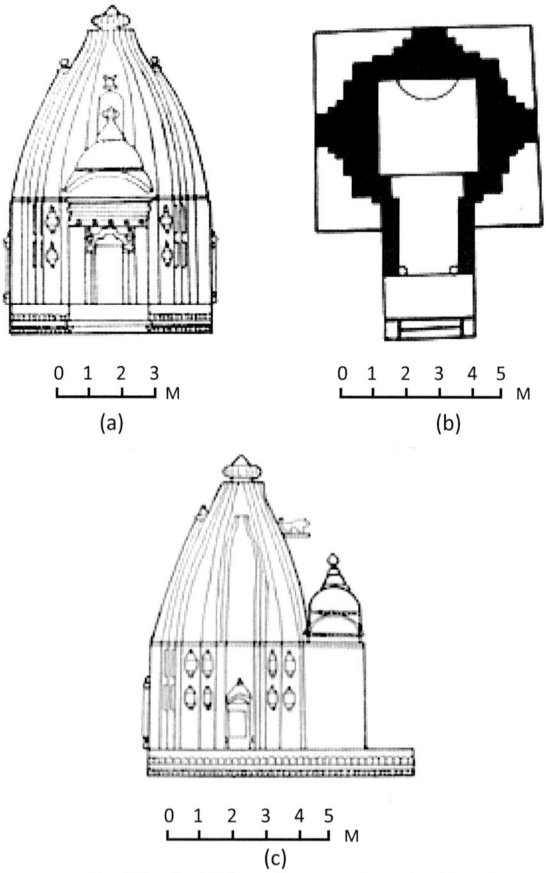

Fig. 9 (a-c) : Mahamrityunjay Temple, Mandi

Mahamrityunjaya Temple: This shrine is located in Thanera Mohalla in the heart of the city. Built in *sikhara* style, it is *pancharatha* on plan facing east, oriented east-west and comprises of a *garbhagriha*, an *antarala* and a porch (Fig. 9 (a-c); Plates 20-21). The *garbhagriha* is square facing east oriented east-west with elevation showing the platform with lotus mouldings topped by *pitha* with *khura* and *kumbha* mouldings followed by lower and upper *jangha* supporting the curvilinear *sikhara* over which is the finial marked by a base, an *amalaka*, a *bijapuraka* and a *dhvaja*.

The *garbhagriha* within has a semi-circular podium, with four-armed stone image of Shiva, Mahamrityunjaya seated cross-legged over a lotus platform. The upper left hand holds a *kalasha* while upper right is in *dhyana-mudra.* The lower left holds a *rudrakshamala* while the lower right holds a rope like snake. The eyes are half closed in meditation wearing ear-rings, locked hair, and upper garments on the body, bracelets in the arms and girdle in the vest. Towards his right below is placed a bronze mast. Besides, there are other religious items placed within the northern and southern walls which have recessed alcoves at centre. The flooring and the walls are veneered with tiles while the ceiling in lantern style has a lotus medallion in the centre.

Externally, the *garbhagriha* walls have lotus mouldings over the platform. The *pitha* has five-tiered mouldings that of *khura, kumbha*, plain pendant and fish-scale from bottom to top. It also shows *bhadra*-niches on south, west and north each containing figures of Hanuman, devotee holding a *gada* and bowl and four-handed Ganesha seated on lotus respectively. The *jangha* portion shows on three sides four miniature niches with *sikhara* on each side of the *bhadra* niches carved in low relief and devoid of figures. However, on the eastern side, the *jangha* wall has only two miniature

Plate 20 : Mahamrityunjaya temple,Mandi

Plate 21 : Mahamrityunjaya temple,Mandi

niches (one on top and another below). The *sikhara* has *amalaka* mouldings on corner *paga* while the central *paga* has two more *pagas* which culminate at half distance and are topped by a finial of *amalaka* and *kalasha*.

The *garbhagriha* is built of sandstone blocks now altered with marble and tiles and plastered externally with lime and coated with oil paint.The rectangular *antarala* is facing east and oriented north-south with elevation showing the platform topped by *pitha* followed by *jangha* supporting the *sukanasika* with *bhadra-mukha* at the centre and placed over it is a figure of tiger. The walls both internally and externally, are devoid of any decoration. The *antarala* could be entered through a stone door-frame showing *matsya* at bottom topped by four *sakhas* carved with floral scroll, human chain standing on each others shoulders, fish-scale and lotus petal respectively from outer to inner side. Only the latter two extend over the lintel. The *lalatabimba* shows four-handed Ganesha figure seated over a pedestal. The flooring is of stone while the ceiling is plain, built of dressed sandstone blocks plastered externally with lime and coated with oil paint.

In front of the *antarala* is a square porch facing east with two pillars at sides. Its elevation shows platform topped by *jangha* walls supporting the domical *sikhara* and finial base, *amalaka,* seven *kalasha* and a *bijapuraka*. The porch internally shows *dvarapala* figure on the north and south walls. The flooring is of marble while the ceiling is in receding rectangles topped by lotus medallion. Externally the *jangha* is plain, topped by low-raised eaves. The domical *sikhara* has arches on three sides interlinked by string course of geometrical motifs. Over the dome is shown an inverted lotus moulding. Its façade shows pillars topped by sage figures within miniature *sikhara* like niches which are intersected by cusped arches with elephant figures on either side. On the top is horizontal panel of floral scroll. It too is built of sandstone blocks plastered both externally and internally with lime and coated with oil paint. Flight of steps is provided towards east of the porch.

Raneshvara Mahadeva Temple: Raneshvara Mahadeva temple is located in the proximity of Kesari Bangla on the left bank of Suketi Khad. The temple is built on a small platform

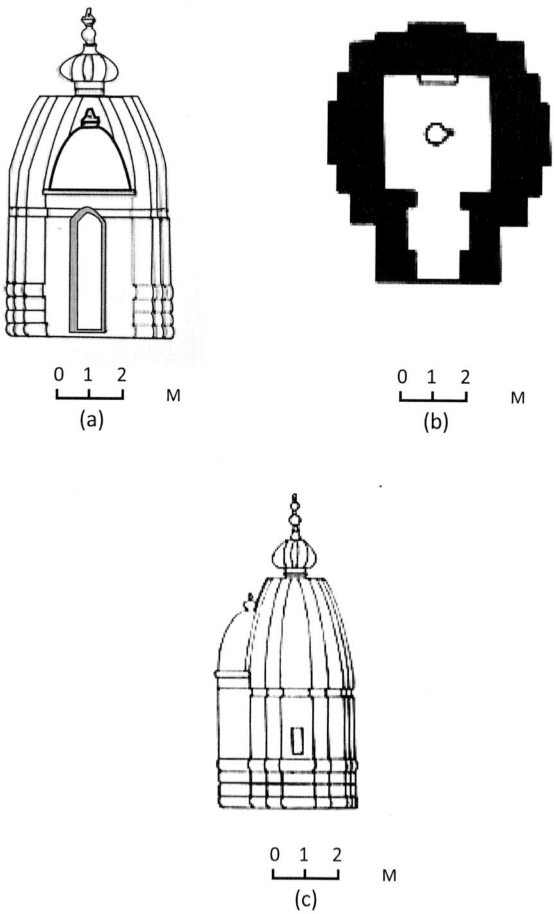

Fig. 10 (a-c) : Raneshvara Mahadeva Temple, Mandi

Plate 22 : Raneshvara Mahadeva Temple, Mandi

Plate 23 : Raneshvara Mahadeva Temple, Mandi

and is approachable through a long flight of steps. Built in typical *sikhara* style, it is *triratha* on plan. Facing north and oriented north-south, it comprises of a square *garbhagriha* and an *antarala* (Fig.10 (a-c); Plates 22-23).

The *garbhagriha* is square facing north with elevation showing the *pitha* and *jangha* supporting the curvilinear *sikhara* topped by an *amalaka*, a cone and *kalasha*. In the *garbhagriha* is the seated image of Trilokinatha with his consort on his lap and a Shiva-*linga* to his front. The other three unidentified figures are on the sides. The flooring and the walls are veneered with tiles while the ceiling is of receding rectangles with lotus medallion in the centre. The façade of the *garbhagriha* shows a *dvarapala* figure on both sides topped by two-tiered door-jamb of floral and fish scale motifs. The *lalatabimba* has a figure of seated Ganesha while the lintel shows floral designs. Externally, the *pitha* mouldings with *khura* and *kumbha* are decorated floral designs while the renovated portion of the *jangha* and *sikhara* are plain.

The *antarala* is a rectangular structure facing north and is oriented east-west with elevation showing the *pitha* and *jangha* supporting the semi-domical *sikhara* topped by finial base, *amalaka* and *bijapuraka*. Its façade has mouldings as in its elevation with lintel showing dancing attendant figures. Internally, the flooring and walls are veneered with tiles while the ceiling is flat and devoid of any decoration. Externally, the *pitha* has *khura* and *kumbha* mouldings while *jangha* is decorated with floral, faunal and human motifs. Two different Nandi figures are shown standing outside facing the temple. The bigger one has a snake below. The base of temple is decorated with green paint, walls have been whitewashed, top of *jangha* and *amalakas* with a shade of golden colour. The whole structure is built of dressed sandstone blocks.

Neelakantha Mahadeva Temple: The temple of Neelakantha Mahadeva is located opposite Mahamrityunjaya temple in the locality of Thanera Mohalla. Built in typical *sikhara* style, it is *pancharatha* on plan, facing east, oriented east-west and comprising of *garbhagriha*, *antarala*, porch and a Nandi platform (Fig.11 (a-c); Plate 24). The *garbhagriha* is square and facing east with elevation showing the platform

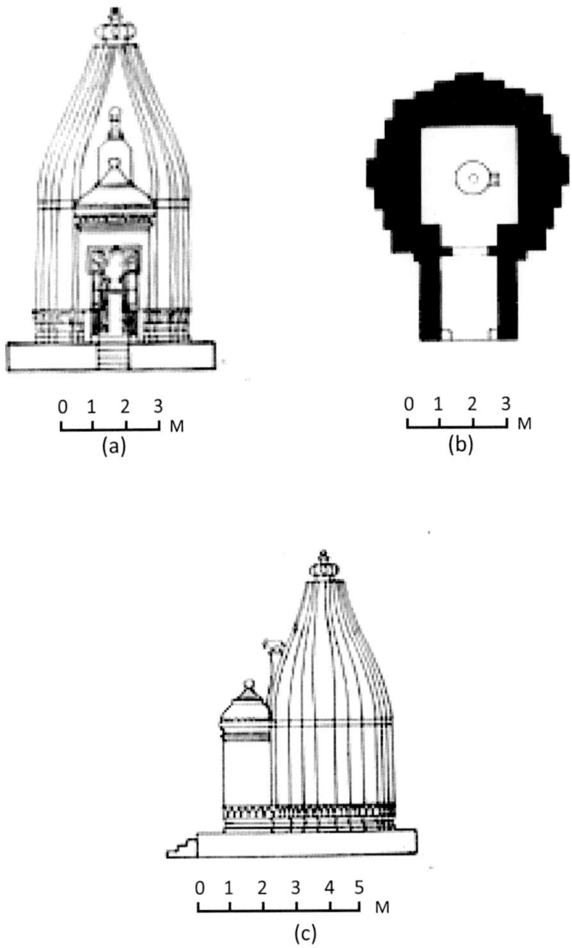

Fig. 11 (a-c) : Neelakantha Mahadeva Temple, Mandi

Plate 24 : Neelakantha Mahadeva Temple, Mandi

over which are the *pitha* and *jangha* supporting curvilnear super structure marked by finial of *amalaka*, *kalasha* and *dhvajastambha*. The *garbhagriha* within enshrines a huge Shiva-*linga* facing north in the centre; the walls are plain with alcoves on west and south. Flooring is of tiles while ceiling is of lantern style topped by lotus medallion. Externally, the whole structure is devoid of any decoration. The platform and *jangha* is plain while the *pitha* shows *khura, kumbha* and *padma* mouldings. The *antarala* is rectangular in plan and is entered through a four-tiered door-jamb with *dvarapala* figure on both sides topped by *sakhas* of floral scroll, *padma* motif, fish-scales and zig-zag respectively.

The figure of Ganesha can be seen on the *lalatabimba*. Internally, it is devoid of any decoration while externally, it is like that of *garbhagriha* with only difference of *sukanasika* with *bhadra-mukha* figure.

Followed by the *antarala* is the square porch with pillars at sides facing east. Its elevation shows the platform topped by *pitha* and *jangha* supporting the domical *sikhara* with finial of *amalaka*s and *bijapuraka.* Its façade is intricately carved with figures of Ganesha, Shiva and Karttikeya on left within niches while the figures of Durga and Brahma are shown on the right within niches. The lower portion of both carry vegetal designs. The pillars are topped by elephant riders and musicians while the lintel shows a battle scene between gods and *asuras*. Internally, the porch is devoid of any decoration. Flooring is of tiles while the ceiling shows receding rectangles with lotus medallion in the centre. Externally, up to the wall portion there are no decorations but the base and top of the dome carry lotus deigns. Standing Nandi on platform is shown facing the temple. The platform is decorated too with lotus design. The whole structure is built of dressed sandstone blocks.

Ramalingeshvara Mahadeva Temple: This temple is located towards west of Ekadasharudra temple and along the complex of Vedanta Kutir Satsang Bhawan. Built in domical style, it is rectangular on plan facing east and is oriented east-west and comprises of a *garbhagriha*, an *antarala*, an open porch and a Nandi platform, all enclosed with a boundary wall (Fig.12 (a-c); Plates 25-26).

(a)

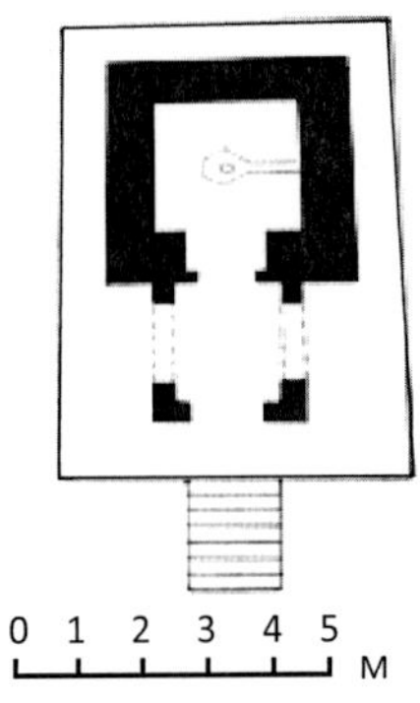

(b)

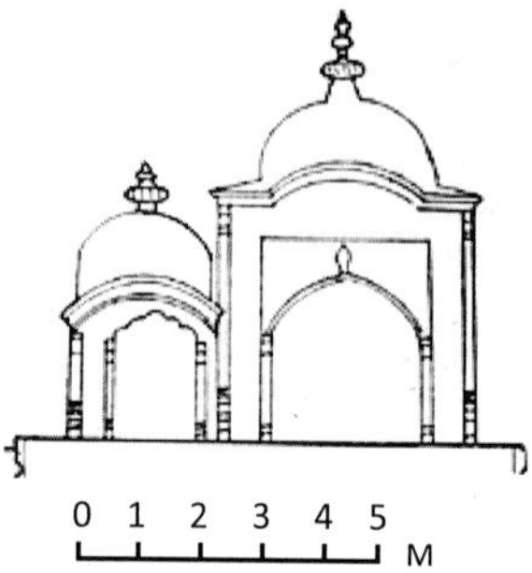

(c)

Fig. 12 (a-c) : Ramalingeshvara Mahadeva Temple, Mandi

The *garbhagriha* is square, facing east, oriented east-west with elevation showing the high platform topped by *jangha* supporting the domical *sikhara* over which is the finial marked by *amalaka*, *kalasha*, *bijapuraka* and *dhvaja*. In the centre is a Shiva-*linga* with *pranala* towards north. The northern wall has niches with figures of Vishnu and Durga on the right and left respectively while the southern wall shows figures of Surya on left and Ganesha on right within niches. The flooring is of marble while the ceiling is in domical shape. Externally, the platform is plain with pilasters on all four corners. The *jangha* walls show in the centre huge niche, low is relief, with cusped arch flanked by pilasters at corners. These pilasters show vase and foliage and lotus designs and have octagonal shaft. On other sides are shown geometrical designs. The *sikhara* is devoid of any decoration. The *garbhagriha* is built of dressed sand stone blocks.

The *antarala* in front of the *garbhagriha* is rectangular on plan, facing east and is oriented north-south with elevation merged from external side. The walls are devoid of any decoraton and can be entered through a plain door-jamb with figure of Ganesha on the *lalatabimba*. The flooring is

Plate 25 : Ramaligeshvara Mahadeva Temple, Mandi

Plate 26 : Ramaligeshvara Mahadeva Temple, Mandi

of marble while the ceiling is of domical shape. Followed by *antarala* is a square open porch facing east with elevation showing the platform topped by pilasters on the back wall and pillars in front interlinked with arch-shaped eaves supporting the domical *sikharas* and finial of *amalaka*, vase and a *bijapuraka*. Internally, it is plain devoid of any decoration. The flooring is of stone while the ceiling is in domical shape. Externally, the pillars and pilasters show motifs of vase and foliage and lotus with an octagonal shaft topped by cusped arches. All around are geometrical designs. The porch is also built of dressed sand stone block. Flight of steps has been provided towards east. In front of the porch is a rectangular Nandi platform with figure of standing Nandi with tail held by a male figure.

Mahadeva Neelakantha Temple: This temple, dedicated to Mahadeva Neelakantha is located on the left side of the old Beas Bridge on NH 20. Built in typical *sikhara* style, it is *triratha* on plan, facing east and oriented east-west. It comprises of a *garbhagriha*, an *antarala*, a porch with Nandi figure and an entrance gate. The *garbhagriha* is square and facing east with elevation showing the *pitha* and *jangha* mouldings supporting the curvilinear *sikhara* and finial of *amalaka*, *kalasa* and cone (Fig.13 (a-c); Plates 27-28).

Within the *garbhagriha* is a Shiva-*linga* facing north at centre while rest is devoid of any decoration. Ceiling is in lantern style. Externally, the *pitha* show *khura*, *kumbha* and *kapota* mouldings while the *jangha* has *bhadra* niches on all three sides depicting a *dvarapala*-like figure on the south, Karttikeya on the west and a composite figure of Matsya and human being on the north. The *sikhara* has *amalaka* mouldings at corners. The *antarala* is very small rectangular in shape oriented north-south with elevations showing the plain *jangha* topped with *sukanasika* carrying *bhadra-mukha* figure.

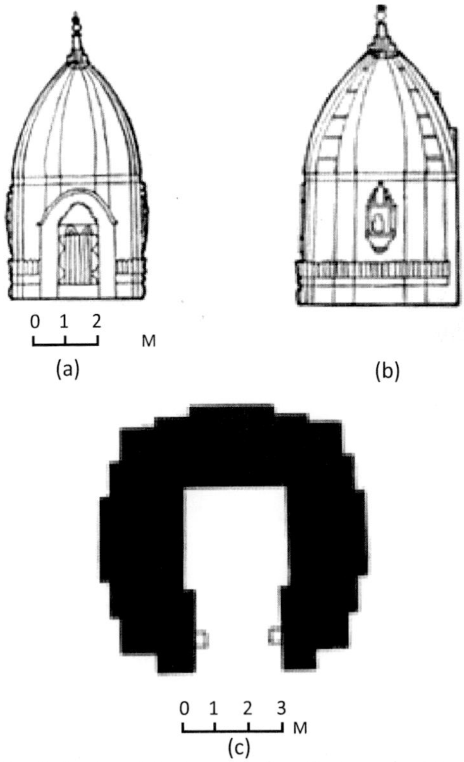

Fig. 13 (a-c) : Mahadeva Neelkantha Temple, Mandi

Plate 27 : Mahaveva Neelakantha Temple, Mandi

Plate 28 : Mahaveva Neelakantha Temple, Mandi

It is entered through a single-tiered plain door-jamb with a *dvarapala* figure on either side topped by floral scroll. The temple is built of dressed sandstone blocks and has now been considerably altered by addition of a modern *mandapa*, tiled entrance way, a small water tank for devotees, extension of courtyard floor with marble stone slabs, etc. and oil painted.

Shiva Temple: This temple is situated at Chhota Tarna just on the way to Shyama or Tarna Devi temple at a distance of about one kilometre from Irrigation and Public Health office. The temple is approachable through a small flight of steps. The temple facing north and oriented north-south has a typical Nagara style of *sikhara.* Built on a high platform and *triratha* on plan, it has a sanctum, an *antarala* and a porch in front (Fig.14 (a-c); Plate 29). The sanctum is surmounted by a curvilinear *sikhara* topped by an *amalaka* and a *kalasa*

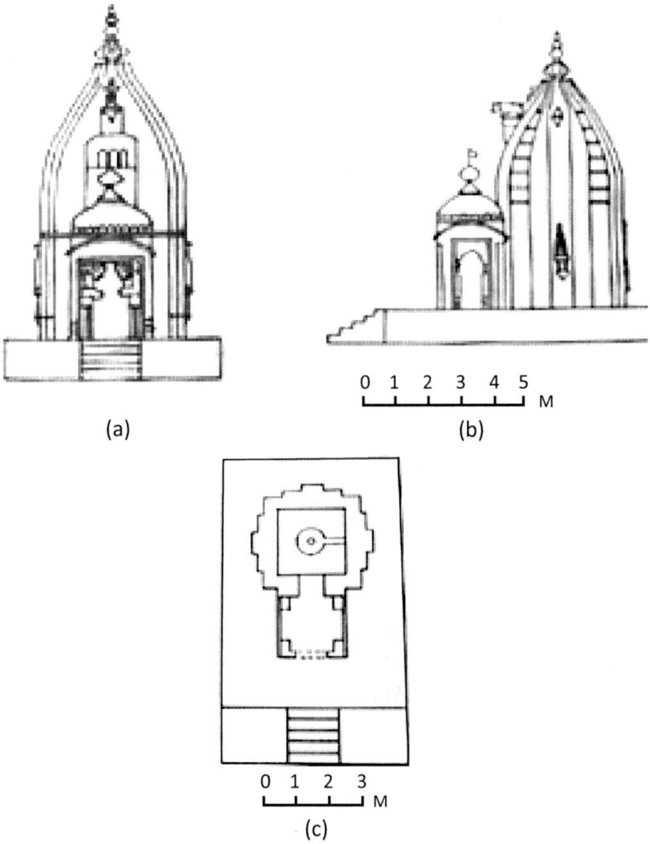

Fig. 14 (a-c) : Siva Temple, Chhota Tarna

finial. The *pitha* comprises of *khura, kumbha* and *padma* motifs while the *jangha* having *bhadra* niches at centre on all three sides has the images of Ganesha, Karttikeya and Brahma on the east, south and west respectively. The finial is marked by an *amalaka*, two *kalasas* and a *bijapuraka*.

The façade and the exterior are devoid of any carvings. Internally, it has tiled flooring while the ceiling is in lantern and domical style topped by a lotus medallion. Shiva-*linga* is shown in the centre of the sanctum and an image of Devi is within the alcove on the back wall. The

Plate 29 : Shiva Temple, Mandi

antarala is a small rectangular chamber with elevation like that of the *garbhagriha* up to *jangha* portion, over which is the *sukanasika* with *bhadramukha* figure and at the top the figure of a tiger. Its façade shows three tiered jamb of floral scroll, lotus petals and fish-scales and a *dvarapala* figure is at the base. The seated figure of Ganesha is shown in the centre of the *lalatabimba*. The porch has a domical member surmounted by similar arrangement of an *amalaka* and a *kalasha* as finial. The façade shows pillars topped by elephant riders followed by cusped arches carrying two musicians, one each on either side. The doorjamb is carved with floral scroll and *dvarapala* at the base. In front of the temple on the ground, but on slightly high platform is placed a Nandi, and a *gana* holding the tail of the Nandi which is a common feature.

Shiva Temple: It is situated on the left bank of Suketi Khad at the confluence point with Beas and Suketi Nala at a distance of about one km from the bus stand towards west.

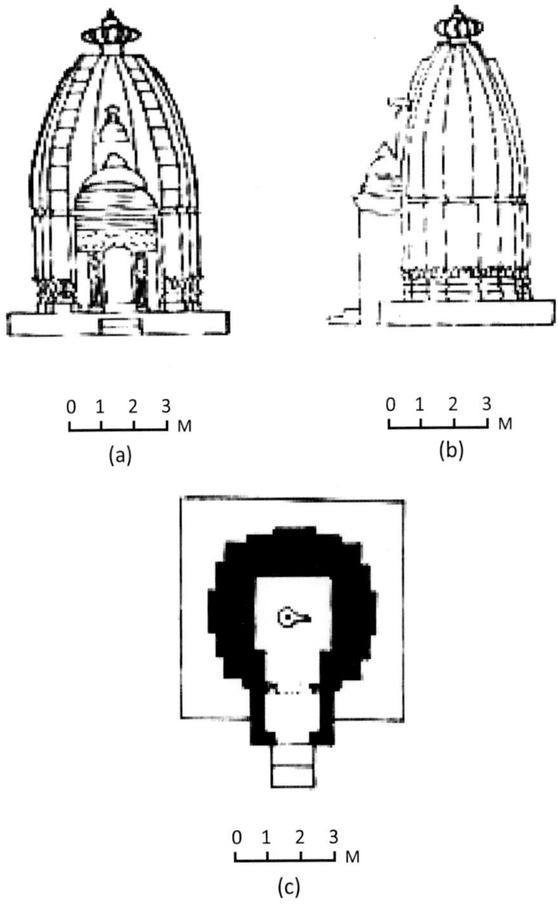

Fig. 15(a-c).Shiva Temple, Mandi

The temple is facing east and oriented east-west. *Triratha* on plan, it comprises of a square *garbhagriha* and a porch in a typical Nagara style (Fig.15 (a-c); Plate 30). The plain exterior has *pitha*, *jangha, sikhara* and a finial made up of *amalakas* followed by *kalasha* and a *trisula*. The ceiling is in typical lantern type. Shiva-*linga* is enshrined in the centre of the sanctum.Ganesha is engraved on the centre of the *lalatabimba* of the lintel. Its *sikhara* is in receding tiers followed by a truncated dome and topped by *kalasha*.

Plate 30 : Shiva and Shani Temples, Mandi

The porch has a rectangular opening at the front with two pillars on the sides and is approached through steps towards east. The pillars have square torus and sixteen-sided shaft over which is floral capital, an abacus and *padma* bracket, the ceiling being plain. On the right is another modern *sikhara* temple dedicated to Shani Deva. A squarish tank with walls on the four sides can be seen towards north-west of the temple. The walls on the west, north and south carry five niches each in bas-relief.

Siddh-Shambhu and Siddh-Kali Temples: These two temples are located in Indira Market of Mandi Town inside the sunken garden with the temple Siddh-Shambhu on the ground floor and that of Siddh-Kali temple on the first floor. These temples were built during the reign of Raja Sidh Sen. These temples are approached through a *torana dvara* from the road level which is much higher than the temple courtyard (Fig.16 (a-b); Plate 31-32). The Siddh-Shambhu Temple, facing north and oriented north-south comprises of a *garbhagriha* and a porch. The *sikhara* is in domical shape while the finial shows an *amalaka, kalasha* and *bijapuraka*. Externally, the *garbhagriha* shows four door openings with

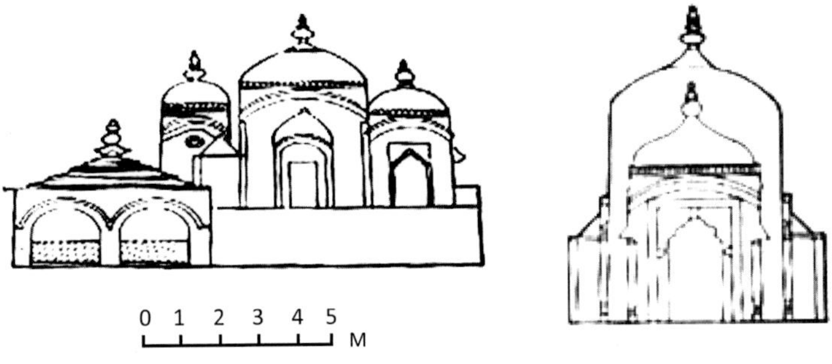

(a) (b)

Fig. 16 (a-b) : Siddh-Shambu and Siddh-Kali Temple

Plate 31 : Siddh Shambhu and Siddh Kali Temples, Mandi

Plate 32 : Siddh Shambhu and Siddh Kali Temples, Mandi

plaster on three sides topped by an arch, a dome and a finial, all carved in low relief. Within the *garbhagriha* are images of Ganesha and Hanumana.

The façade shows pilasters on the side of the door-jambs which is in three tiers of floral scroll, lotus petals and fish scales. Seated Ganesha is shown in the *lalatabimba* topped by lintel showing friezes of floral scrolls. Internally, it shows tiled flooring and roof with domical type. The images of Nandi, a mouse, a buffalo and a tiger are placed over a platform and topped by Shiva-*linga*.While the Siddh-Kali temple is rectangular on plan and facing south and oriented north-south, it comprises of square *garbhagriha* and a *mandapa* and built of sandstone blocks and plastered externally. On elevation, it shows a low raised platform over which are the walls with window openings at sides followed by a domical *sikhara*-like that of Siddh-Shambhu temple. The image of Kali is within the alcove. While the *mandapa* is a modern attachment and its elevation shows platform over which are the pillars followed by a flat roof and a finial. Internally, it has a tiled flooring and a tapering ceiling and devoid of any decoration. Architecturally, the temple shows a blend of classical traditions and rural and folk ethos on one hand, and elements of plains, especially use of stunted dome as superstructure over the sanctum on the other hand.

There is a small *havan kund* (fire altar) in front of the entrance to the temple. Dedicated to goddess Kali, the temple is visited by a large number of devotees at the time of *aarti.* The temple is under worship. At present it is painted with various colours. A little less than a life-size standing image locally known as Siddh Bhairava has been placed towards an edge of the Sunken Garden of the Town (Plate 33). The image is in blue-colour, two-armed holding a *nagapasa* (noose made of a snake) going round his neck

Plate 33 : Standing image of Siddha Bhairava

with protruding eyes, possible wreath of skulls (?), wearing a crescent moon on his forehead, and lower parts clad in lion-skin. The image appears to be a copy of wooden prototype.

Shiva Temple: This temple is located on the left side of the bridge connecting the old and the new Mandi at a distance of about one kilometre from the bus stand. Approach to the temple is through a flight of semi-circular steps. Facing east and oriented eastwest, it comprises of a *garbhagriha* and a porch in typical *nagara* style with *triratha* plan on a high platform of sandstone blocks (Fig.17 (a-c); Plates 34-35).

It has a square *garbhagriha* with a *pitha, jangha, sikhara* and finial at its elevation. The finial comprises of double

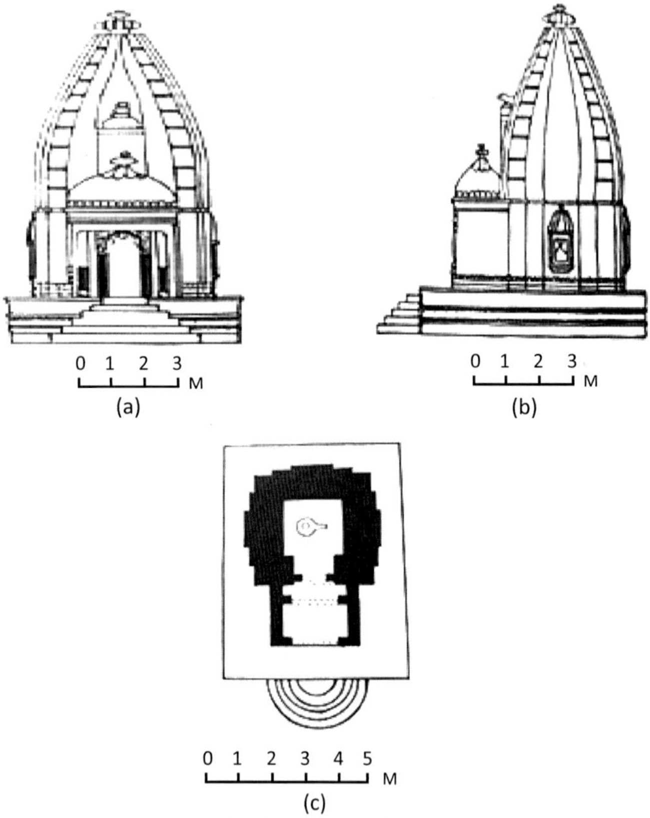

Fig.17 (a-c) : Siva Temple, Mandi

amalaka followed by hemispherical dome topped by *trisula.* The pillars have a *ghatapallava* torus, a sixteen-sided shaft and a floral capital. Both the pillars are linked with floral arches. The ceiling is in diminishing squares with a central rosette. The façade with various floral mouldings carry the figure of Ganesha. Shiva-*linga* is enshrined in the sanctum. On the exterior within the three arches of the central *rathas* are figures of Garuda towards south, Brahma on the west and a eight armed male deity seated on a crouching lion on the north. This figure carries on right from top to bottom a *gada,*

Plate 34 : Shiva Temple, Mandi

Plate 35 : Shiva Temple, Mandi

khadga, abhayamudra and a lamp while on the left from top to bottom is a *trisula, damaru,* shield and in *varadamudra.* The lion holds in the right a *khadga* and on the left a shield. The lion is shown with face of animal and the body in human form.

The porch is somewhat squarish with two pillars each on either side. Its pillars are exactly similar like that of the *garbhagriha.* The ceiling is divided into three blocks with the central one carrying diminishing rectangles. Nandi is shown on a raised platform in a standing position in front of the temple.

Dugleshvara Mahadeva Temple: This temple is located near Dhunglighat on the left bank of the river Beas and to the right side of the old bridge at a distance of about a kilometre west of the Mandi bus stand. The temple is facing north-east and oriented north-east-south-west. It is rectangular in plan and comprises of a *garbhagriha,* an *antarala* and a porch (Fig.18 (a-c); Plates 36-37). The *garbhagriha* is square facing south-east and is raised on a platform with a pilaster on each corner. The elevation shows *pitha* followed by *jangha, sikhara* and a finial. The *pitha* has mouldings of *khura, kumbha* and lotus while the *jangha* has niches on all sides.The *sikhara* is domical while the finial carries an *amalaka* and capped by *bijapuraka.* Externally, the *jangha* shows figures of Varaha, Narasimha and Hanumana in the niches on the south, west and north respectively. Besides these niches, there are on either side plain niches flanked by pilasters at corners.

Internally, it has cement flooring and the ceiling is domical with receding tiers and lotus medallion in the centre. Shiva-*linga* is enshrined in the *garbhagiha.* The other images in the sanctum are that of Ganesha, Mahakala, Durga and Surya. The *antarala* is rectangular, facing north-

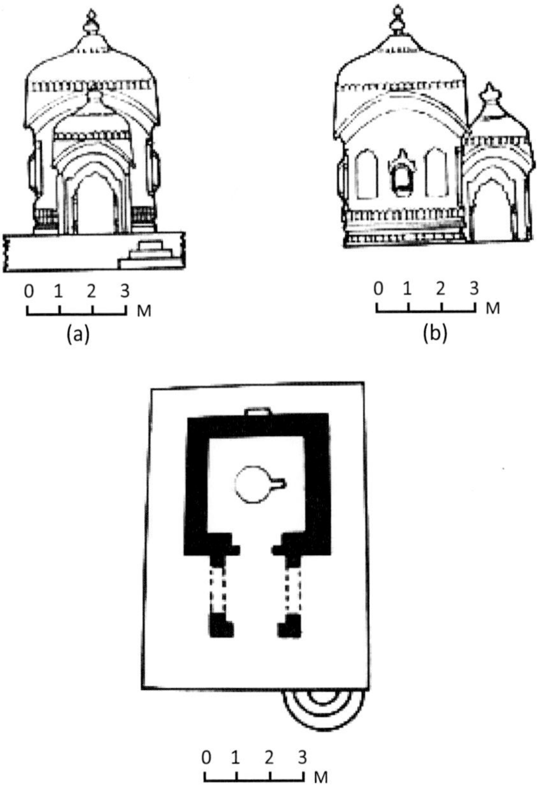

Fig.18 (a-c) : Dugleshvara Mahadeva Temple, Mandi

east with elevation showing a platform over which is the *pitha* and finial marked by a figure of tiger. Its façade shows *dvarapala* at the bottom topped by three-tiered plain door-jamb while the *lalatabimba* shows a seated Ganesha. The interior is devoid of any decoration.

The porch is square on plan and open on all sides; its domical roof is supported on pillars. The finial is marked by a base, an *amalaka* and *bijapuraka*. Externally, the pilasters at the corners are decorated with floral designs while the domical *sikhara* shows lotus on top as well as at the bottom.

Plate 36 : Dugleshvara Mahadeva Temple, Mandi

Plate 37 : Dugleshvara Mahadeva Temple, Mandi

Internally, it has stone flooring and plain walls devoid of any decoration while the ceiling has lotus medallion in the centre. The façade is also without any decoration. Within the temple compound there are plenty of loose sculptures among which mention may be made of Parashurama, Gauri-Shankar, Kali, Rama-Lakshmana, Sita, Ganesha and Hanumana, etc. A standing figure of Nandi is placed over a platform in front of the temple.

Small Monolithic Temple: This temple is located in Paddal Mohalla, located on the confluence of the Beas river and Suketi Nala and close to Panchavaktra temple. This small monolithic rock-cut temple is a rare relic of great antiquity and the image is symbolically represented as *linga* on a *yoni-pitha* encircled by *naga* on a plain and square sanctum. On the jambs, *dvarapalas* are depicted standing in attendance (Plates 38-39).

Plate 38 : Monolithic rock-cut shrine, Mandi

Plate 39 : Monolithic rock-cut shrine, Mandi

Siddh Sambhu Mandir: Located on the left side of the Beas river in Paddal Mohalla, this monolithic rock-cut shrine represents a Shiva-*linga* in the centre of a *yonipitha* at the base, both fashioned as if resting upon a small platform. It was built by Raja Sidh Sen. Nandi is shown seated at the base of the platform. It is being maintained by the local priest and the small area around has been enclosed with boundary wall and providing local grey sandstone flooring to the open courtyard (Plates 40-41).

Plate 40 : Siddh-Shambhu rock-cut sculptures, Mandi

Plate 41 : Siddh-Shambhu rock-cut sculptures, Mandi

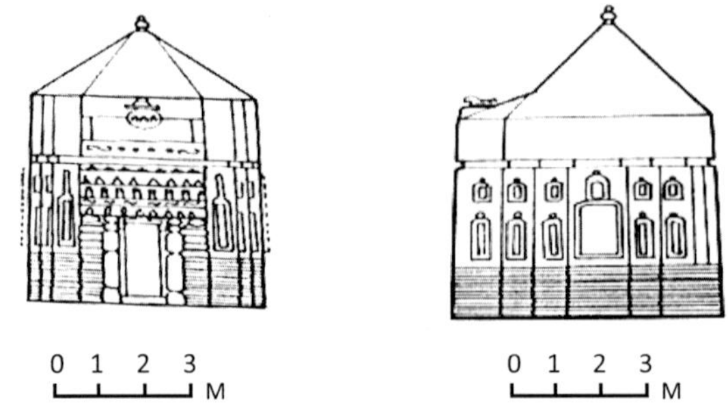

(a) (b)

Fig. 19 (a-b) : Mahakala Temple, Mandi

Mahakala Temple: Towards east of the Shiva-Deula (Bijali Mahadeva) temple at a few distance on the left bank of the Beas river near the Hanuman Ghat is located this temple (Fig.19 (a-b); Plates 42-44). It is said that before the dead is consigned to the fire the pyre is brought here to offer *pinda*, one of the last rites of the dead.Built of sandstone blocks and facing north and oriented north-south, it is *tri-ratha* on plan. It comprises of a *garbhagriha* and an *antarala* in typical Nagara style. However the original *sikhara* appears to have been rebuilt by giving a stout and tapering shape.

Plate 42 : Mahakala Temple, Mandi

Plate 43 : Mahakala Temple, Mandi

Plate 44 : Mahakala Temple, Mandi

The *garbhagriha* is square on plan and has in its elevation *a pitha, jangha, sikhara* and *kalasha* and a miniature cupola. The ceiling is in receding square tiers topped by rosette in the centre. Externally, the *pitha* shows six different types of mouldings covered with lotus petals followed by floral scrolls, miniature *sikharas* and floral patterns or scrolls. The lower *jangha* portion carries a central *bhadra* niche flanked by two other niches on either side hosting the figures of musicians.

The upper *jangha* shows a *bhadra* niche on the south and a miniature *sikhara* type niche on the east and west respectively. The *sikhara* is curvilinear with the central *ratha* showing an arched *sikhara* with *bhadramukha.* The second *ratha* shows cut lines while the third *ratha* shows *amalakas* intersected by *chaitya* motifs.

The façade shows attendant figures at the base topped by four-tiered door-jamb with Ganesha shown on the *lalatabimba* which is also topped by six heads in a row. Internally the *garbhagriha* shows plain cement flooring while the ceiling is in receding squares topped by a lotus medallion.Within the *garbhagriha* is enshrined an image of five-headed and ten-armed Shiva seated over Nandi with Uma on his lap. His ten arms hold in left from top to bottom a shield, *damaru*, embracing Uma and *kamandalu*, a snake and a flower while on the right arms from top to bottom *abhayamudra*, *trisula*, a vessel, *rudraksha-mala* and *kartari.* The *antarala* is a small rectangular chamber facing north and oriented east-west with two pillars at its sides. The door-jamb has lotus at upper corners while the lintel shows a series of thirteen miniature *sikharas* followed on top by a row each of floral scrolls, dancers and musicians, floral scrolls and petals and topped by a *bhadramukha.*

Guptesvara Mahadeva Temple: This temple is located near Siddh Ganapati temple in Sain Mohalla. The temple is *sikhara* type, having a polygonal base and a single cella as sanctum, above which rise curvilinear *sikharas* in successive offsets. In front of the temple is placed Nandi, the mount of Shiva. It is also under worship and heavely decorated with oil-bound/enamel dark red paint alternating with yellow colour concealing the original features of the temple.

Kameshvara Mahadeva Temple: This rectangular shaped temple is located very close to the old bus stand (Plate 45).

Plate 45 : Kameshvara Mahadeva Temple, Mandi

This temple is dedicated to Kameshvara Mahadeva, for fulfilment of desire (*kama*). Desire is one of four canonical efforts, *dharma, artha* and *kama* and it is believed that by worshiping Shiva as Kameshvara, one can seek fulfillment of desires and overcome delusions. As one would judge from the surviving examples, these are the temples which show impact of the plains, since while on the one hand they have retained just a few of the classical features like *garbhagriha* and *mandapa, pradakshina-patha* and *torana.*

The *sikhara* is replaced by a dome over the sanctum. It is built on a raised platform and has a sanctum and ambulatory with arched openings towards roadside. It has big pillars supporting the roof. In the sanctum sanctorum is the Shiva-*linga*.

Bhatanti Mahadeva Temple: The Bhatanti Mahadeva temple is located near the Bhawani Palace and is a private temple of the Raja of Mandi, entry to which is restricted to general public for viewing. The temple is opened on very special occasion or some special auspicious day or on such festive days as are considered appropriate by the owner of the temple. Here Mahadeva is shown with eight-arms holding trident, skullcup, drum, mace, flower, rosary and serpents. Its sculptural excellance is remarkable and unique as it looks fresh and new.

(B) Shakti or Devi Shrines

Sitala Mata Temple: The temple of Sitala Mata is located in Purani Mandi at a distance of about 250 m from Trilokinath Temple towards north-east. Built in typical *sikhara* style, it is *triratha* on plan facing south-south-west and comprises of *garbhagriha,* an *antarala* and a porch (Fig. 20 (a-c); Plates 46-47). The *garbhagriha* is square with podium at back wall and faces south-southwest with elevation showing a platform over which is the *pitha* followed by *jangha* supporting the curvilinear super structure topped by the finial of a base, an *amalaka*, a disc, a *kalasha*, *bijapuraka* and a *dhvaja*. Within the *garbhagriha* in the centre is the stone image of Sitala Mata who is shown in standing posture holding in left hand a *kamandalu* while the right one is in *varada-mudra.* Two female attendants holding a broom and basket are shown on top. The bronze mask on the face and two upper bronze hands are later additions. Other figures are that of Mahishasurmardini, Ganesha and Hanumana on

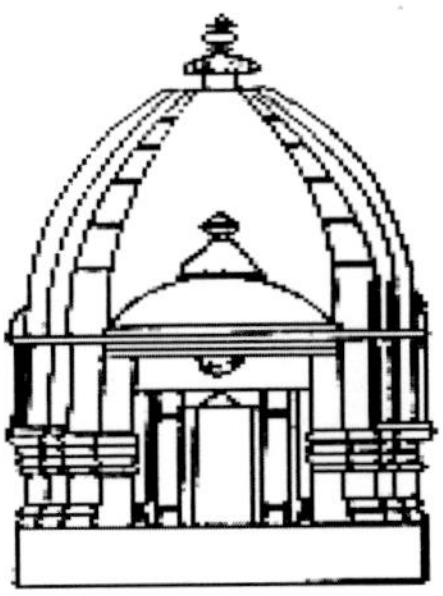

0 1 2 3 M

(a)

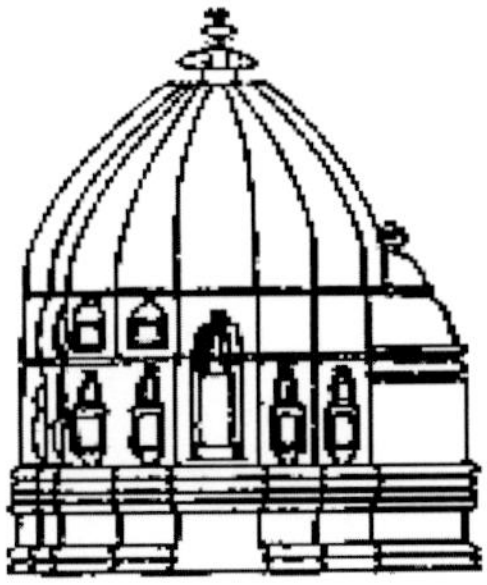

0 1 2 3 M

(b)

0 1 2 3 M

(c)

Fig. 20 (a-c) : Sitala Mata Temple, Mandi

her right and Mahishasurmardini, Bhadrakali and *pindi* on the left. The walls are devoid of any decoration except for a frieze of *hamsas* with tiger faces at corners on the top and two miniature *sikhara*-like niches on the eastern and western walls. Flooring is of marble while the ceiling is in lantern style with central lotus medallion. Externally, the platform is of wooden style and devoid of any decoration. The *pitha* shows *khura* and *kumbha* mouldings followed by a gap and then horizontal friezes of respectively of floral scroll followed by elephant and *hamsas*, then plain circular and finally by lotus petals. The *jangha* shows a huge central niche in the *bhadrapaga* flanked by two niches each on either side on both the upper and lower *janghas*. Rest of the space in the *jangha* show floral and geometrical designs. There are no figures present within any of the niches. The *sikhara* is plain

Plate 46 : Sitala Mata Temple,Mandi

Plate 47 : Sitala Mata Temple,Mandi

with only *amalaka* mouldings at corners. The *antarala* is rectangular in plan and is entered through a door-jamb with each side topped by five *sakhas* namely from inner side-geometric, four musicians and a Mahishasurmardini figure on either side within niches; fish-scale motif and finally lotus petals.

Four-armed seated Ganesha is shown in the centre of the *lalatabimba.* Its flooring is plain while the ceiling is in arch style. These walls are also oil painted. The *antarala* is followed by rectangular porch with two pillars and two pilasters in front facing south-south-west. Its elevation shows platform over which is the *pitha* followed by *jangha* supporting the twin domical *sikhara* topped by finial of a *kalasha* and *bijapuraka.* Its façade shows floral, faunal and geometrical designs with a three-headed *bhadra-mukha* figure over the *lalatabimba.* The pillars show *chaitya* arch and diamond motifs followed by circular shaft with top decorated in zig-zig designs, and the square bracket capital is decorated with *ghata-pallava* designs. The pilasters, on the other hand, show *dvarapala* figure below topped by lotus medallion and vase and foliage motif. The flooring is of stone while the ceiling is in lantern style with the first tier decorated with faunal designs while the second one shows lotus motif within niches. The whole structure is built of dressed sandstone blocks mortared within clay and oil painted.

Mata Chintapurni Temple: The temple of Chintapurni (Mandir Shree Mata Chintapurni Annapurna) is located in the same congested market of Mandi town on the same road in which the temples of Bhutnatha and Shree Balakrupi are situated. The temple is dedicated to Chintapurni. It is a small temple, but now substantially altered with marble flooring in the courtyard, modern tile work on the walls, while the walls and door-frame are decorated with thick oil bound/ enamel paints. In the surroundings of the temple, there are many modern constructions thereby changing the original landscape. The temple, facing north-west and oriented south-east is rectangular in plan comprising of a *garbhagriha*, an *antarala* and a modern *mandapa* with *pradakshinapatha* (Fig. 21 (a-b)).

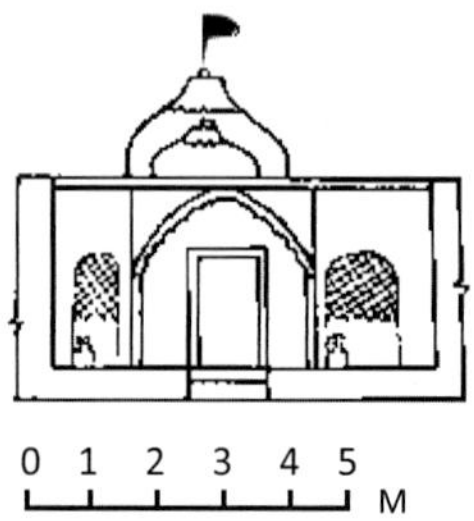

(a)

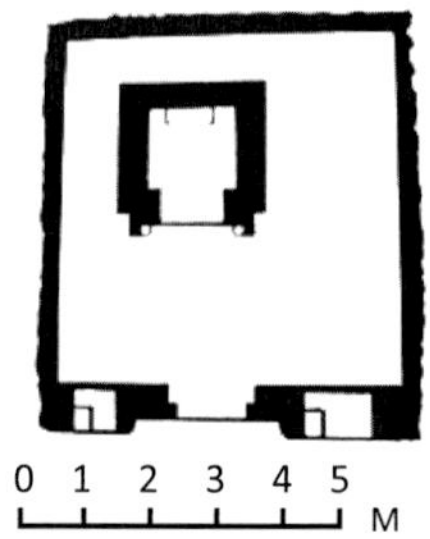

(b)

Fig. 21 (a-c) : Mata Chintapurni Temple, Mandi

It has a square *garbhagriha*. Internally, the flooring is of cement while the ceiling is square and receding with tapering roof topped by lotus medallion. It has the image of Mata Chintapurni and others flanked by few loose sculptures. On elevation it has plain *pitha, jangha, sikhara* and finial. The *jangha* shows niches on three sides devoid of any figure.The *sikhara* is domical while the finial is broken. Its façade shows door-jamb with five-tiers that of floral scroll, lotus petals, fish scales, etc. The *antarala* is a small rectangular chamber with pillars on sides. The pillars are composed of circular *ghata* topped by sixteen-sided fluted shaft and a square capital flanked by walls with *dvarapala* at the base and topped by floral scrolls. Seated figure of Ganesha is shown in the *lalatabimba*.

Durga-Maheshvara Mahadeva Temple: The temple, also known as Durga Maheshwara Mahadeva temple, is located within Bhagwan Mohalla near open platform. Built in *sikhara* style, it is rectangular in plan, facing south, oriented north-south and comprising of *garbhagriha* and a *mandapa*. The *garbhagriha* is square in plan, open from three sides and faces south with elevation showing the platform over which are pillars in front with wall only towards north supporting the curvilinear *sikhara* topped by a finial of base, *amalaka*, *kalasha* and core (Fig. 22(a-b); Plate 48).

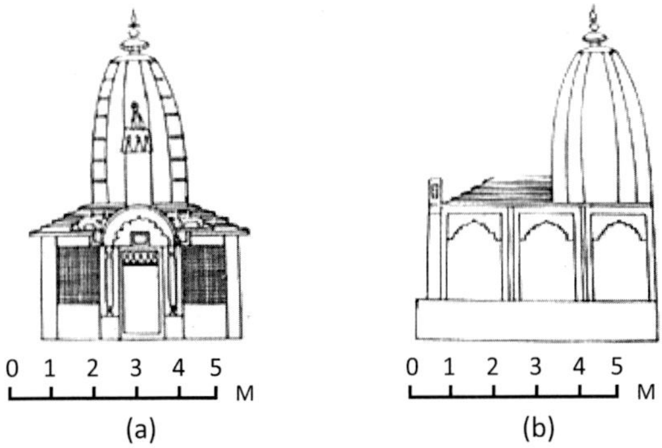

Fig. 22 (a-b) : Durga Maheshvara MahadevaTemple, Mandi

Plate 48 : Durga Maheshvara Mahadeva Temple, Mandi

The *garbhagriha* has a stone figure of Mahishasurmardini placed over a throne in the centre and flanked by two Shiva-*lingas* at right facing north and Panchavaktra Maheshvara Mahadeva figure towards left. Flooring is of marble while ceiling is of domical shape. Pillars are interlinked with arches. Externally, the platform and the wall are devoid of any decoration while the *sikhara* carries a *bhadra-mukha* figure on top towards south. *Amalaka* mouldings are decorated with floral designs. The *mandapa* enclosing the *garbhagriha* from three sides is rectangular in plan facing south, oriented east-west with elevation showing the platform over which are the walls supporting the flat pyramidal roof with parapet wall towards south.

Within the *mandapa* can be seen figures of Hanumana and Kali placed inside niches towards west and east respectively. The flooring is of tiles while the ceiling is tapering shape meets the top of the arched dome of *garbhagriha*. Externally, the whole structure is plain except the niches which are in low relief with cusped arches. The *mandapa* has a plain door-jamb with figure of Ganesha over the *lalatabimba*. The whole structure is built of dressed sandstone blocks plastered internally and externally with cement.

Bhuvaneshvari Devi Temple: The temple of Bhavaneshvari Devi is located near the present Municipal Committee office and opposite Sabzi Mandi in Mahajan Bazar and was built by Raja Bhawani Sen. The temple preserves an admixture of classical and folk elements, integrating architectural ideoms of north Indian plains as can be seen in domed superstructure in place of a *sikhara.* It is octagonal in plan facing south-east, oriented north-west-south-east and comprises of a *garbhagriha*, an *antarala* and a porch. The *garbhagriha* is square facing south-east with elevation showing the *pitha* and *jangha* portions supporting the domical *sikhara* and finial marked by an *amalaka*, a *kalasha* and a *bijapuraka* (Fig. 23 (a-b); Plate 49).

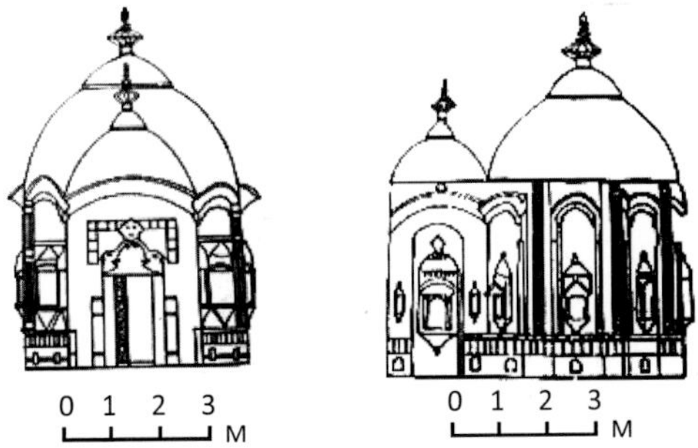

(a) (b)

Fig.23 (a-b) : Bhuvaneshvari Devi Temple, Mandi

Plate 49 : Bhuvaneshvari Devi Temple, Mandi

It enshrines a four-armed bronze image of Bhavanimata, about three feet in height. The goddess is shown seated on a stone pedestal with right leg hanging down and the lower right hand in *abhayamudra* while lower left in *varadamudra.* The upper both hands are found empty but poised in the act of holding some attributes without *vahana.* The head is provided with a small *mukuta*, the central one is shown little higher from the others. The flooring is of tiles while the ceiling is in domical shape. Internally, it is devoid of any decoration. Externally, the *pitha* shows *khura*, *kumbha* and lotus mouldings while the *jangha* at all octagonal sides has a miniature *sikhara*-like niche topped by a Takri inscription and an arch. Between two niches is a pilaster while rest of the space is decorated fully by floral designs. A frieze of floral scroll can be seen between the junction of *pitha* and *jangha.* The *sikhara* is devoid of any decoration. Between the *garbhagriha* and the porch is the rectangular *antarala* facing south-east while its exterior is merged with the porch. It can be entered through a door-frame showing *dvarapala* figure at the bottom topped by a four-tiered jamb of floral scroll, lotus petal, zig-zag and floral scroll respectively.

A seated figure of Ganesha is shown over the *lalatabimba* while the lintel is decorated with floral scroll. Internally, it is devoid of any decoration. In the front is the square porch with two pillars at front and elevation showing the *pitha* over which is the *jangha* supporting the domical *sikhara* and finial of base, an *antarala*, two *kalashas* and *bijapuraka.* Attendants and deities are shown in the horizontal and vertical friezes at places. Inside, the flooring is of tiles while the ceiling is of receding squares with lotus medallion in the centre. The remaining portions are devoid of any decoration. The present temple was built by Raja Bhawani Sen (1903-12) under the inspiration of Jai Dev Upadhayay, a Sanskrit scholar. This tradition is still alive in Mandi to name the deity with the name of the Raja who caused the creation of its idol or construction of its temple.

Jwala Mata Temple: This temple is located adjacent to the Mandi Police Station building near the *mela* ground. Built in *sikhara* style, it is rectangular on plan facing east, oriented east-west and comprises of a *garbhagriha*, *pradakshina-patha* and a *mandapa* (Fig. 24 (a-b); Plates 50-51).

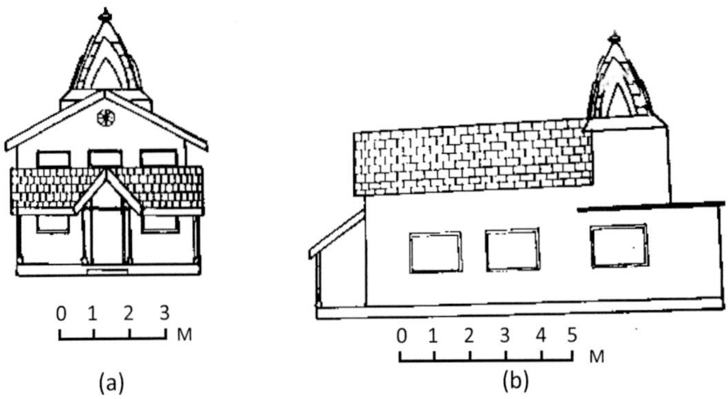

Fig. 24 (a-b) : Jwala Mata Temple, Mandi

Plate 50 : Jwala Mata Temple, Mandi

Plate 51 : Jwala Mata Temple, Mandi

The *garbhagriha* is square, facing east, with elevation showing the platform over which are raised the walls, with window openings on the north and south, supporting the curvilinear *sikhara* and finial of a base, an *amalaka* and a *bijapuraka*. It has inside a figure of Jwala Devi seated on a lion over a throne. The flooring is of cement while the false ceiling is of wood. Externally too it is devoid of any decoration. In the front and enclosing the *garbhagriha* is the rectangular *mandapa* facing east, oriented east-west with elevation showing the platform over which are the walls with window openings supporting the chalet-styled roof. Internally and externally, it is devoid of any decoration. The flooring is of cement while the false ceiling is of wood. A figure of tiger facing the temple is seen in front of the *mandapa*. The platform and the walls are of dressed stone blocks while the roof is of slate stone. This temple was reconstructed by Shri Yashodhara Singh on 21st July, 1948.

Jalpa Mata Temple: The temple of Jalpa Mata is located on the left bank of the Beas river in Purani Mandi. Built in domical style, it is rectangular on plan facing north-west, oriented south-east-north-west and comprises of *garbhagriha*, an *antarala* and a modern *pradakshina-patha* (Fig. 25 (a-c); Plates 52-53).

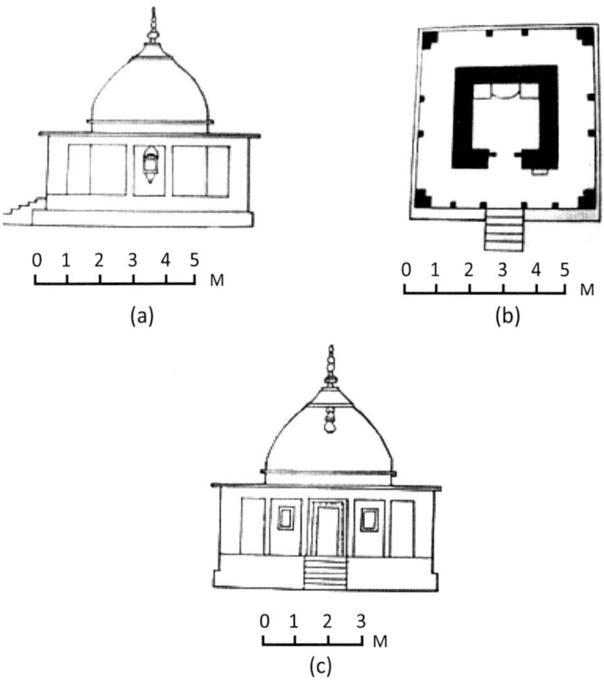

Fig. 25 (a-c) : Jalpa Mata Temple, Paddal, Mandi

The *garbhagriha* is square facing north-west with elevation showing the platform over which is the *pitha* and *jangha* supporting the domical *sikhara* and finial marked by an *amalaka*, three *kalasha*s and *bijapuraka*. The *garbhagriha*

Plate 52 : Jalpa Mata Temple, Mandi

Plate 53 : Jalpa Mata Temple, Mandi

is entered through a three-tiered door-jamb decorated with floral scroll and followed by four vertical panels of deities each. The lintel shows seated Ganesha on the *lalatabimba* flanked by other deities at sides. The *garbhagriha* has within two stone podiums in the corners which carry a frieze of attendants with lions at corners.

Over the left podium is the figure of Jalpa Mata and two other unidentified deities while on the right podium are figures of Durga, Ganesha and Hanumana. The flooring is of cement while the ceiling is of domical style with lotus medallion in the centre. Externally, the platform is devoid of any decoration. The *pitha* has *khura* and *kumbha* mouldings while the *jangha* portion shows a single niche on three cardinal directions. The *sikhara* dome shows lotus design at the base and top. In the front of the *garbhagriha* is the rectangular *antarala* facing north-west oriented north-east-south-west with elevation showing the platform over which is the *pitha* and *jangha* supporting the *sukanasika*. It can be entered through a plain door-jamb flanked by a niche at both sides with figure of Hanumana on right. Internally, it is devoid of any decorations while externally the platform is plain while *pitha* shows *khura* and *kumbha* mouldings. Enclosing the *garbhagriha* and *antarala* is a pillared *pradakshina-patha* square in plan with two pillars each at centre of three sides and four pillars at centre of south-western side. Besides these, two pillars have been provided at corners. It is completely devoid of any decoration. In the front of the temple complex is a standing figure of tiger facing the temple. The *garbhagriha* and *antarala* are built up of dressed sandstone blocks while the *pradaksina-patha* is built of bricks and RCC.

Jalpa Devi Temple: Jalpa Devi temple is located near Divisional Forest office, Purani Mandi, and is situated on the right side of NH 20. Built in domical style, it is square on plan facing west oriented east-west and comprises of a *garbhagriha* and an enclosed *pradakshina-patha* (Fig. 26 (a-c)).

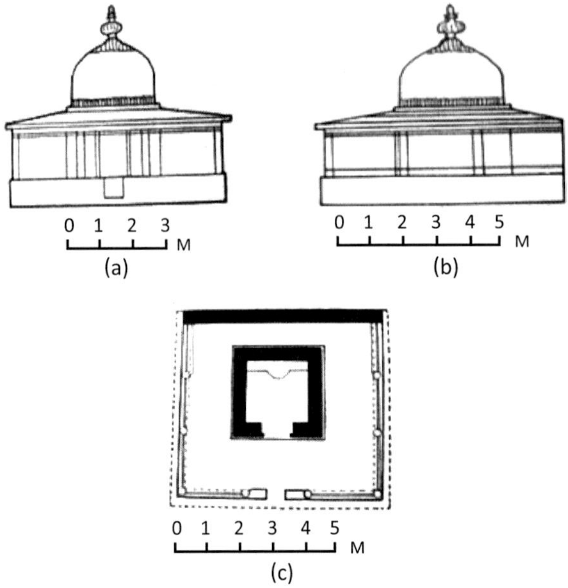

Fig. 26 (a-c) : Jalpa Devi Temple, Mandi

The entablature with slanting superstructure and over extending eaves is devoid of any decoration. A figure of a tiger is placed on out side in front of the temple. The whole structure is built of stone and bricks and plastered both internally and externally with cement and coated with lime.

Bangleshvari Mahadeva Temple: Located within Bangla Mohalla and associated with *tantric* form of worship, it is a small temple raised on a low platform and has a small step in the shape of *chandrashila* with a sanctum and a small covered *mandapa*. Built in typical *sikhara* style, it is rectangular in plan, facing west and oriented east-west. The *garbhagriha* is square facing west with elevation showing a platform over which is the *jangha* supporting the curvilinear *sikhara* topped by finial of two *amalaka*s and *bijapuraka* (Fig. 27 (a-b)).

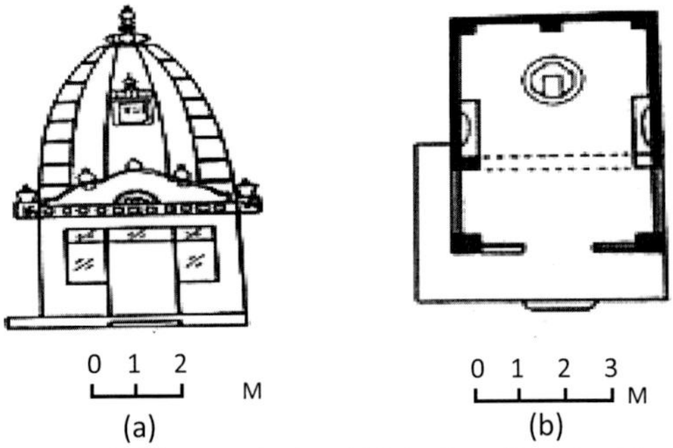

Fig. 27 (a-b) : Bangleshvari Mahadeva Temple, Mandi

The *garbhagriha* hosts the bronze figure of a female deity placed within a *sikhara*-like platform. Figures of Rama, Lakshman and Sita are shown on the northern wall and that of Hanumana on the southern wall. A Shiva-*linga* can be seen to the front of Hanumana. Flooring is of marble while walls are veneered with tiles, the ceiling is in domical style. Externally, the platform and *jangha* are plain while the *sikhara* is decorated with *amalaka*s at corners. Parapet of the *jangha* has floral and geometrical designs to the front of central *bhadra paga* are a *bhadra-mukha* within rectangular frame. The porch is rectangular in plan facing west oriented north-south with elevation showing the platform over which are the walls with flat roof and arched parapet wall towards west. It is devoid of any decoration both internally and externally and shows marble flooring and plain flat ceiling. The whole structure is built of stone and plastered externally.

Tarna Mata or Shyama-Kali Temple: Shyama-Kali temple also called the temple of Tarna Mata, is situated about three km from the centre of the town in Sanyarti Mohalla. The approach to the temple is from the main bazar through about 305 stairs. It was built on the Tarna Hill overlooking the town of Mandi during the reign of Raja Shyam Sen in 1659 CE to commemorate his victory over Suket and annexation of Bahl area to Mandi state. The temple facing north-west and oriented south-east-north-west is a typical *Nagara*-cum-domed style temple. *Triratha* on plan, it comprises of *garbhagriha* and *pradakshina-patha* (Fig. 28 (a-b); Plate 54).

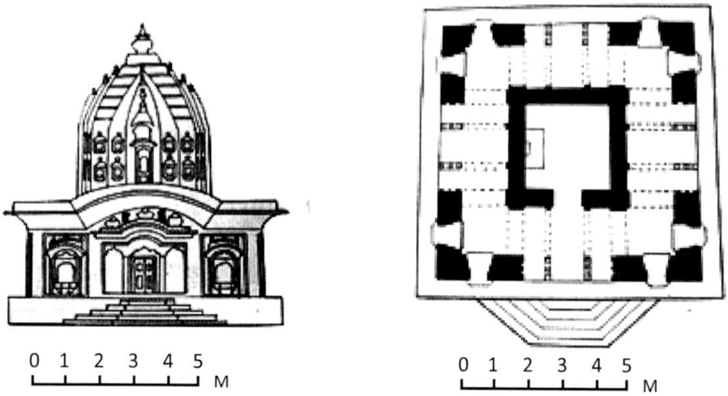

(a) (b)

Fig. 28 (a-c) : Shyama-Kali Temple, Tarana Hills

Plate 54 : Shyama Kali Temple, Mandi

The *garbhagriha* is square and facing north-west and built of stone blocks plastered and oil painted externally. The elevation shows a raised platform with *khura, kumbha* and *khura* mouldings followed by *jangha* with decorated pillars at corners and *bhadra ratha* topped by *sikhara* and four miniature *sikhara*-like projections on all sides with a finial on the top. The façade of the *garbhagriha* is divided into three parts by pilasters; the central part carries the doorway while on the left and right are painted forms of goddess Mahakali and Tara respectively. Internally, the walls are decorated with applique work and other semi-precious stones. Within the *garbhagriha* is the image of three-faced Kali in black stone on a decorated pedestal. The other loose images are that of Hanumana, Vishnu standing on *matsya*, Karttikeya, Mahishasuramardini, Shiva-*linga,* Shiva-Parvati, etc. The ceiling is also decorated with paintings in gold and silver colour. The *pradakshina* is an open pillared square chamber with arched openings on all four sides.

The external walls of the *garbhagriha* have now been decorated in oil paint with images of Devi in her various tantric forms – ten Mahamayas, Mahakali with Shodasi, Bhuvaneshvari, Chhinnamasta, Tripura Bhairavi, Dhumavati, Baglamukhi, Kali, Kamala, Matangi and Tara. The temple is also linked to Raja Balbir Sen (1839-1851 CE) who spent many years at the Sikh court as prisoner, but who is said to have renovated and embellished the temple after his release. During Navaratri days in the month of *Aasuj,* all children of the royal family are taken there for ceremonies which are performed eight days after birth.

Bhimakali Temple: This temple is located on the right bank of the Beas River near Beas Sadan on the right side of Bihuli bridge on the Mandi-Pathankot National Highway. It is one among the most important temples in Mandi town and dedicated to goddess Bhima Kali (or Bhimakali). The temple from outside appears an architectural marvel which is most recent in date. However, the modern structure conceals inside it a relatively old temple; portion of an earlier sanctum, which has now been altered due to modern construction. Presently renovated in pyramid shape, it is square on plan facing north, oriented north-south comprising of a *garbhagriha* and a *pradakshina-patha* while its elevation shows walls in three storeys followed by pyramidal *sikhara* with rising gradually on different slopes (Fig. 29 (a-b); Plates 55-56). The *garbhagriha* with *pradakshina-patha* finds place on the topmost storey while the lower three stories host enclosed pathway leading upwards.

The *garbhagriha* is square, facing north, oriented north-south with elevation showing the walls with flat roof. The *garbhagriha* hosts a stone image of Bhimakali Devi in the centre placed over a platform while the Shiva-*linga* is on the right, Ganesha on the left, Mata Devi and Nainadevi in front. The flooring is of marble while the walls are veneered

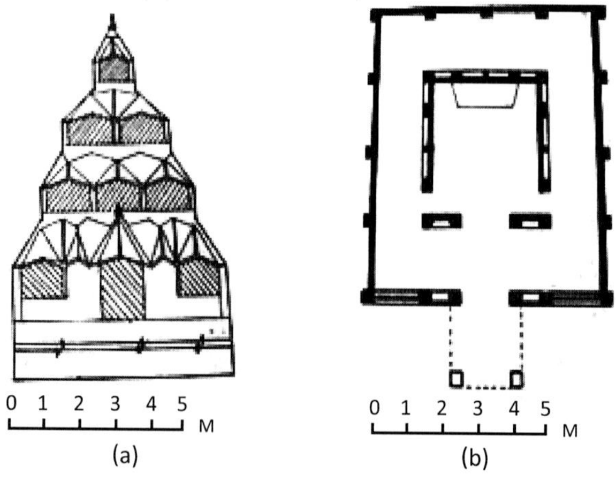

Fig. 29 (a-c) : Bhimakali Temple, Mandi

Plate 55 : Bhimakali Temple, Mandi

Plate 56 : Bhimakali Temple, Mandi

with glass and the flat ceiling is of wood. On the external side of the walls of *garbhagriha* are figures of various forms of Kali namely Mahakali, Tara and Shodasi towards east, Bhuvaneshvari, Chhinnamasta, Sritripura-bhairavi and Dhumavati towards south and Baglamukhi, Matandi and Kamala towards west.

The *pradakshina-patha* is also square in plan, facing north with elevation showing open pillared balconied walls topped by extended eaves with pyramidal *sikhara* and finial comprising two *amalaka*s and four brass *kalasha*s. It is devoid of any decoration internally while externally tiles have been used.

The approach pathway facing the bottom three floors/ storey has a figure of Hanumana mounted on wall towards north while abraded ancient sculptures are placed along the western wall.

A Shiva-*linga* has been placed towards the *kund* on the north-west facing north. It is rectangular in shape with a *pranala*. The temple is renovated form of earlier existing stone temple and is presently built up of cement blocks decorated in white and ochre colours.

Chamunda Mata Temple: The Chamunda Mata temple is located in the School Bazar at a distance of about one and half km from the bus stand. Facing west, this temple is in rectangular in plan and comprises of a *garbhagriha* and a *mandapa.* The *garbhagriha* is square and facing west with elevation showing the *pitha* followed by *jangha*, a curvilinear *sikhara* and a finial marked by a base, an *amalaka*, a *kalasha,* three discs and *bijapuraka*.

Internally, it hosts a standing image of Chamunda in the centre. The sanctum is fronted by a rectanglular *mandapa* which is covered with a flat roof, and surmounted by a small

Plate 57 : Chamunda Mata Temple, Mandi

Plate 58 : Chamunda Mata Temple, Mandi

Plate 59 : Chamunda Mata Temple, Mandi

pyramidal *sikhara*. It is a later newly addition to the temple. The figures of two lions are guarding the passage leading to the temple. A miniature shrine with an image of Bhairava is kept on the left and the image of Hanumana on the right outside the temple (Plates 57-59).

Sitala-Mata temple: The temple of Sitala Mata is located in the area of Somkhetar. Built in domical style, it is oblong in plan facing south-east oriented north-west-south-east and comprising of a *garbhagriha* only. Its elevation shows the walls supporting the domical roof while rest is under construction. It can be entered through a façade of modern door flanked by window opening. This portion would also be reconstructed soon. It hosts a stone image of Sitala Mata with silver mask placed over a throne decorated in *sikhara* style. The other deities present are: Balasundari, Taradevi, Baba Balak Guru, Chamunda, Hanumana, Ganesha, Shiva-*linga* and *pada* besides a Tiger, respectively. Rest is devoid of any decoration. The temple was earlier of stone but is now rebuilt in bricks and RCC.

Khua Rani Mandir: The Khua Rani Mandir (or Queen of the Well Temple) is situated on the left bank of the Beas river in Samkhetar Mohalla (Patwar Circle) of Mandi town. It is a small temple built inside a rectangular pond-like stepped-well (*baoli*), covered with wooden roof. The water table has now gone so deep that it has disappeared totally. In older times, the *baoli* must have been serving the people with its plentiful potable water. According to one belief, this well celebrates the time when Princess Mandarava, the Princess of Zahor or Sahor (identified with Mandi), became a consort of Padmasambhava. The temple thus became sacred to both Hindus and Buddhists. Being located in the heart of dense urban setting, the temple is under worship and has been made modern.

Rupeshvari Devi Mandir: The Rupeshvari Devi Mandir is located near the old Maisahiba royal enclosure, now Raj Mahal Hotel and is also a private shrine of the Rajas of Mandi. The entry to the shrine is restricted to the general public for viewing but is opened on special occasions or on such festive days as are considered appropriate by the owner of the temple. The idol of eight-armed Devi is shown seated on a silver pedestal in *bhumisparsa-mudra* and wearing jewelled crown on the forehead. She is also wearing nose-ring and *yantra* in the throat. She is shown holding in each arm trident, *chakra*, lotus, dagger, shield, noose, etc. The idols of Markandeya and Ganesha are on either side of the deity.

Rai Rajeshvari Devi Mandir: The Rai Rajeshvari Devi Mandir, located within Damdama premises, is the presiding deity of the Rajas of Mandi, the entry to which is restricted to general public but it is opened on special occasions on auspicious or on festive days as are considered appropriate by the owner of the temple.

Kangni Mata Mandir: This shrine is located at Kangni Dhar. This small temple has a flat roof with covered varandah in front of the sanctum. It has three small pyramid-shaped *sikharas* surmounted by *kalasha*-like finials. The temple is under worship.

Parkash Dei Mandir: The Parkash Dei Mandir located within the Damdama Palace, is a private temple of the Rajas of Mandi, entry to which is not allowed to general public for viewing. The temple is opened on a very special occasion on some special auspicious day or on such festive days as are considered appropriate by the owner of the temple.

Mahishasuramardini Mandir: This temple is located at Bhagwan Mohalla within the multi-storied modern structures. This is a small temple with a sanctum and a covered *mandapa*; the sanctum is surmounted by a *sikhara* having a *kalasha* on the top finial which appears to have been reconstructed at some later date. In the sanctum is enshrined an image of Mahishasuramardini which is of a very late date. The four-armed stone image is shown riding on a lion and holding in her arms trident, sword, *khappar* and shield. Image of Panchvaktara and Shiva-*linga* are kept in the corners of the sanctum. The inner flooring is of marble slabs. The temple is under worship and is heavily painted with oil-bound/enamel paint of pink, red, golden and other colours.

(C) Vaishnava Shrines

Radha-Krishna Temple: The temple of Radha-Krishna is located in Purani Mandi area near market place. Built in *sikhara* style, it is square on plan and facing east. It comprises of a *garbhagriha* only (Fig. 30 (a-c); Plate 60).

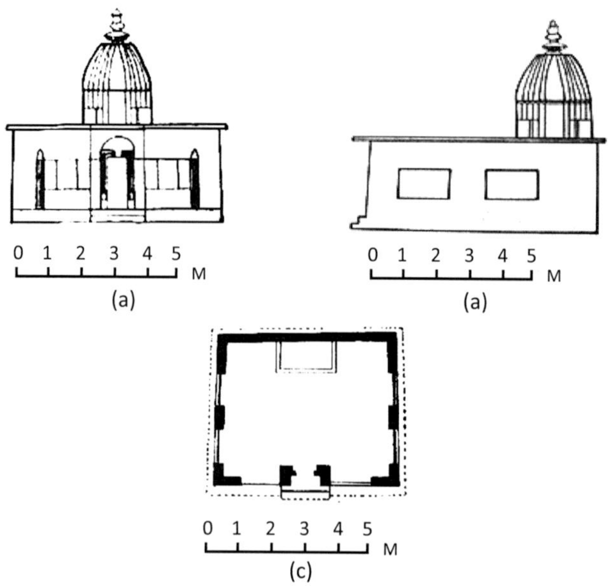

Fig. 30 (a-c) : Radha-Krishna Temple, Purani Mandi

Plate 60 : Radha-Krishna Temple, Mandi

Its elevation shows a low-raised platform over which are the plain walls with two window openings at north and south, supporting the flat roof with curvilinear *sikhara* at centre towards west representing the *jangha* and *sikhara* form of a temple followed by a finial marked with an *amalaka*, *kalasha*, *bijapuraka* and *dhvajastambha*. It can be entered through a façade showing a door-jamb flanked by window openings and pilasters. The door-jamb has a *dvarapala* figure at centre over which are three-tiers respectively of lotus petals, fish scales and geometric pattern. The *garbhagriha* hosts a marble figure of Radha and Krishna enclosed within a square stone podium. Towards their right is a figure of Vishnu with consort seated over Garuda in stone within a niche. Externally, it is devoid of any decoration. The entire temple is built of bricks mortared and plastered with cement and belongs to a modern date.

Sita-Rama Radha-Krishna Temple: Sita-Rama Radha-Krishna temple is located in Purani Mandi and is situated on the west of Sitala Mata temple. Built in domical style, it is square on plan facing east oriented east-west and comprising of a *garbhagriha*, an *antarala* and an open porch. The *garbhagriha* is square, facing east with elevation showing the plain platform topped by *pitha* with *khura* and *kumbha* mouldings followed by a *jangha* supporting the domical *sikhara* over which is the finial marked by a base, an *amalaka* and *bijapuraka* (Fig. 31 (a-c)). It hosts an *ashtadhatu* image of Sita-Rama and Radha-Krishna placed over a pedestal and a Shiva-*linga* with *parnala* towards north in the centre of the northern wall. Single niche on each wall shows a seated Ganesha on the western wall, four-armed Panchavaktra Shiva seated over Nandi on north and Shiva-Parvati seated over Nandi on the southern wall.

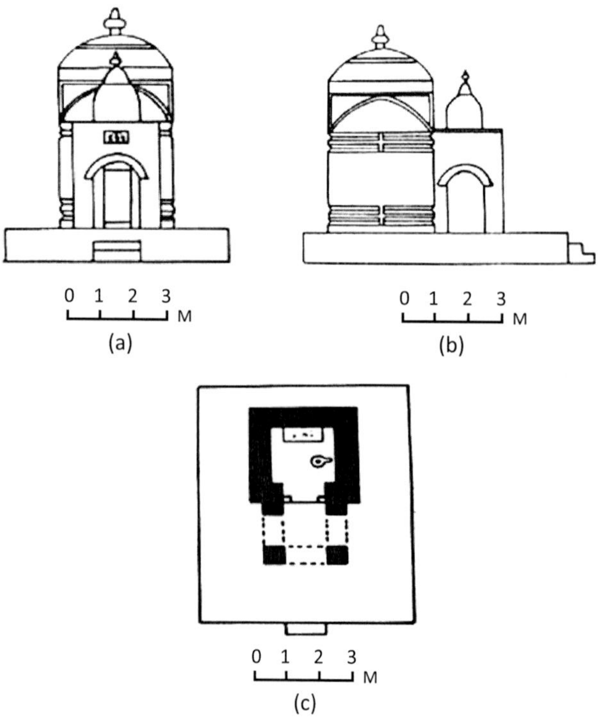

Fig. 31 (a-c) : Sita-Rama Radha-Krishna Temple, Mandi

The flooring is of marble while the ceiling has its base in lantern style with top in domical fashion. The *antarala* is rectangular on plan facing east and is entered through a plain three-tiered door-frame with a *dvarapala* on either side while the *lalatabimba* shows two-handed seated figure of Ganesha over mouse eating *laddoos*. Followed by *antarala* is a square open porch facing east oriented east-west with elevation showing the platform topped by pilasters on the back wall and pillars on the front interlinked with arches supporting the domical *sikhara* topped by finial of base and *amalaka*. Its façade shows a three-headed *bhadra-mukha* on top. Inside it the flooring is of stone blocks while the ceiling is in lantern style. Pilasters are decorated with lotus designs while the pillars are plain. The whole structure is built of dressed sandstone blocks now plastered with cement and white-washed.

Jagannatha Temple: The Jagannatha temple, located in Paddal Mohalla of Mandi Town, is an ordinary *sikhara* type temple and built on a raised platform amid multi-storied modern constructions. Entry is through an arched entrance, a long open passageway and somewhat long flight of steps. This temple was built or established by the Raja Gur Sen in 1679 (Plates 61-62). On plan, the temple comprises a sanctum and a *mandapa* which has cement flooring. The wooden image of lord Jagannatha is enshrined in the sanctum, which was brought by the Raja Gur Sen back from his travel from Puri. The temple is under worship and entire temple structure is painted with oil-bound/ enamel paint of yellow, red and other colours.

Madho Rai Temple: The Madho Rai Temple is located on Post-office road adjoining the office of the Deputy Commissioner of the District and it has its own history. This temple is one of the famous temples of the Mandi town. It

Plate 61 : Jagannatha Temple, Mandi

Plate 62 : Jagannatha Temple, Mandi

is said that the Raja Suraj Sen married several times but was not fortunate enough to be blessed with an heir–apparent and as such in consultation and with the advice of his court astrologers and other religious scholars, he abdicated his kingship to the God Madho Rai, a form of Vishnu. He spent rest of his life as his regent and representative. The Raja assigned the State to the deity which is still the object of highest veneration by the people of the Mandi and the royal family. It is Madho Rai too who gives Raj Tilak to every ruler of Mandi. The Madho Rai temple occupies the greater part of the lower storey of the Damdama old palace which was built by Raja Suraj Sen. The image is placed on a silver pedestal over lotus-shaped marble base in the sanctum sanctorum. The inscribed silver idol of lord Madho Rai was made by one Bhima in the year 1648 CE as revealed from the Sanskrit text of the inscription. The inscription records that

> "Surya Sen, the lord of the earth, and destroyer of his rivals, had this blameless image of the blessed discus-bearer and master of all the gods, the illustrious Madho Rai, made by Bhima the goldsmith, in the year Vikaram 1705, on Thursday, the 15th Phagan."

This date corresponds to March, 1648 CE. The figure of Radha-Krishna is shown engraved in the main silver pedestal. On the entrance are engraved celestial nymphs, elephants, birds, flowers, creepers, etc. The other figures engraved in the entrance gate are Krishna playing flute, cows, Ganesha with Ridhi and Sidhi, Siva-Parvati riding on Nandi, etc. It is said that this temple is very popular for holding and celebrating International Shivaratri festival and Holi festival. All the gods and goddesses from different parts of the state come in state processions and pay due respect and honour to the Madho Rai.

Sanatan Dharma Sabha: The Sanatan Dharma Sabha is located in Bhagwan Mohalla within the school complex. This totally renovated modern structure is rectangular in plan facing south, oriented north-south and comprising of three square *garbhagrihas* (numbered 1 to 3 from left to right) and a common pillared *mandapa* flanked by rooms at both sides for residential and other purposes. General elevation shows that it is double-storied and has three shrines (Fig.32 (a-b);

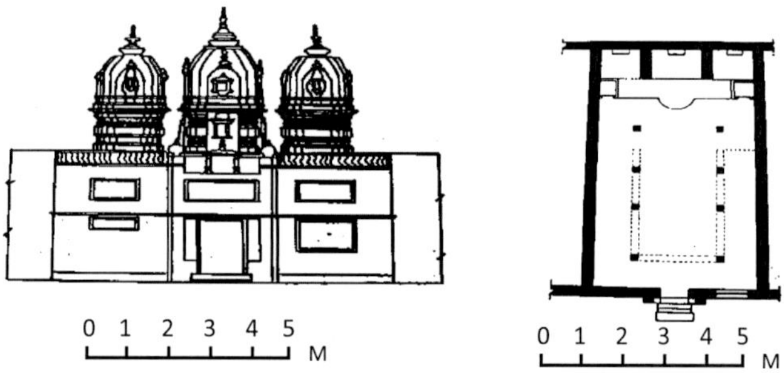

(a) (b)

Fig. 32 (a-b) : Sanatan Dharam Sabha, Mandi

Plate 63 : Sanatan Dharam Sabha, Mandi

Plate 63). In the sanctum of the first shrine is contained a figure of Radha-Krishna placed on a podium while the figures of Rama, Lakshman, Sita, Bharata, Shatrughna and Hanumana are kept in the second shrine. The images of Shiva and Shakti are enshrined in the third shrine. Figures of Ganesha and Durga can be seen in the hall placed at left and right respectively within small shrines. Façade of shrines show cusped arches with central portion depicting elephant heads flanked at sides by lotus designs while in the second shrine it carries musicians instead of lotus design.

Externally, all the three shrines are identical comprising of *jangha* with multi-mouldings for supporting the curvilinear *sikhara* topped by finial marked by abacus, *amalaka*, lotus, *kalasha* and *bijapuraka*. The central *bhadra paga* facing south shows figures of Hanumana and Shiva within niches of shrines two and three respectively while the niche of first shrine is shown blank.

The other three *bhadra paga* facing north, east and west carry a lotus design each. The *mandapa* is rectangular in plan facing south, oriented north-south with eight pillars supporting the corridor of the upper storey thereby forming aisle below. Both internally and externally it is devoid of any decoration. Pillars are also plain. The whole structure is built of dressed sandstone blocks mortared and plastered with cement. The superstructure however is of red sandstone.

(D) Other Shrines

Baba Balakrupi Temple: Located in the same congested market of Mandi town on the same road on which the Bhutnatha temple is situated, this temple is one of the famous temples dedicated to Baba Balakrupi Natha. The temple facing south-east and oriented north-west-south-west is irregular in plan. Built two-storyed, it comprises of a square *garbhagriha* and a *pradakshina-patha* and an office on the ground floor while another office is at the top floor with a curvilinear *sikhara* on the terrace and a finial marked by an *amalaka, kalasha, bijapuraka* and *dhvajastambha* (Fig. 33 (a-b); Plates 64-65).

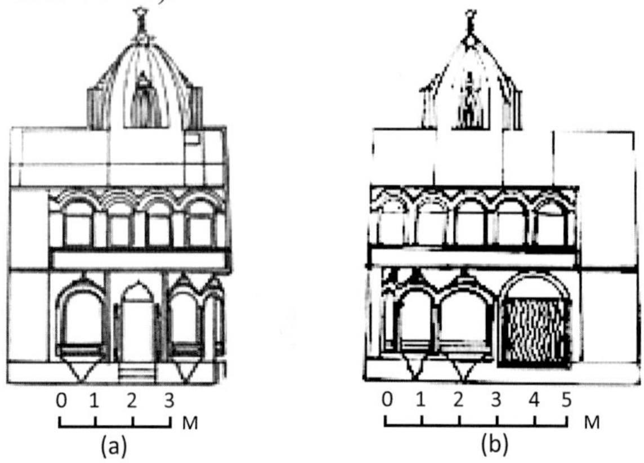

Fig. 33 (a-b) : Baba Balakrupi Temple, Mandi

Plate 64 : Baba Balakrupi Temple, Mandi

Plate 65 : Baba Balakrupi Temple, Mandi

In the centre of the *garbhagriha* is the Shiva-*linga* along with a marble image of Shiva kept in the front of the *linga*. The *pradakshina* is also an irregular structure with elevation showing a platform over which is the wall with window openings towards south-east and north-east.

This temple could perhaps be ancient but now it has been substantially altered with marble flooring done in the courtyard, and walls and door-frames decorated with thick oil bound/enamel (polymer) paints which have interfered almost irretrievably with its original look entirely.

Siddh Ganapati Temple: This temple is located in Sain Mohalla near Regional Hospital on the Mandi-Kotla road. Built of sandstone blocks, it is square in plan and facing south-east and oriented south-east and north-west. It comprises of sanctum-sanctorum only (Plates 66-67). The elevation shows that it was built on a terraced raised hill followed by

Plate 66 : Siddha Ganapati Temple, Mandi

Plate 67 : Siddha Ganapati Temple, Mandi

a *pitha* with *khura, kumbha* and *padma* motifs, *jangha*, a domical *sikhara* on square, octagonal and circular base and topped by a finial of *amalaka*. The façade shows a plain door-jamb flanked by pilasters with figure of Ganesha in the centre of the *lalatabimba.* Above it is an eave with projected rafter-like mouldings in stone. Internally it is plain and hosts a huge four-armed image of Ganesha, seated in *padmasana* over a lotus platform. He is shown carrying *rudraksha-mala*, a *parasu*, and *rudraksha-mala* in his hands. The mouse is seated on his right. A stone life-size image believed to be of Raja Sidh Sen can still be seen in this temple. There are few loose sculptures in the sanctum. The flooring is of tiles while the ceiling is in domical shape. This temple was built during the reign of Raja Sidh Sen.

Babakot Mandir, Damdama: The Babakot temple is located in one corner room of upper storey of Damdama Palace. It is also a private temple of the Rajas of Mandi. Made of wood, this small temple is now opened for public only on Sundays. In the corner of the room are enshrined image of Babakot. There are many legends associated with this temple and is venerated by offering tobacco in any form of cigarette or *huqqa* (hubble-bubble). The devotees believe that if the presiding deity is propitiated, the deity is powerful enough to fulfil devotee's all mundane wishes. The idol is seated on a stone pedestal and wearing garlands of snakes. His head is decorated with embellished crown and wearing spotlessly white garment. He is shown riding on a horse. He is shown wearing ear-rings in the ears like those of *nath-yogis*, and wooden footwear in his feet. He is holding trident and skull-cup in his hands. Other image is seated Narasimha who is wearing sacred thread and rosary in his hand.

(E) Other Monuments

Barsela Monuments: The custom of erecting stone pillars, like tomb stones, as memorials to the dead was regarded as royal privilege and prevailed all over the inner hills particularly in Mandi, Suket and Kullu. These pillars are only rough slabs set on end with very stylized representation of the deceased. In Mandi, these slabs are found having ornamental carvings with inscription in Takri characters and dated in the *lok-kala* or era of the seven *rishis*. In all, there are about one hundred and fifty royal memorial stones slabs commemorating the Rajas of Mandi and common men; these still stand in a group on a plot within walled enclosure at Mangwain locality near the bank of the Suketi river (Plates 68-69). These pillars are locally known as *barselas*.

Plate 68 : Barsela monuments, Mandi

Plate 69 : Barsela monuments, Mandi

The figures of respective Raja and his queens/*ranis* and concubines who sat on the dead Raja's burning pyre were carved on these stone slabs. Some of these are six or seven feet high. As many as twenty-five women died with one particular Raja. In one of the earlier *barselas* in the upper panel the Raja is shown worshipping a *linga*; the lower panel depicts females of the household according to their status. Some of the memorials are having inscription in Takri script.

The inscriptions engraved on them record the name of the Raja and the date of his death as well as also the number of queens, concubines and slave girls. William Moorcraft visited Mandi in 1820 and mentioned that he had seen several memorial stones, constructed in the memory of the queens and other women, who became *sati* along with their royal husband. These are 6-7 feet high and are carved with figures of *rajas* and *ranis* who became *sati*. In addition to the queens, many *khwasis* and *rakhails* (keeps) were also immolated with the *rajas*. For instance, with Raja Shyam

Sen alone, who died in 1679 CE, five *ranis*, two *khwasis* and 87 *rakhails* were immolated. According to the figures given by Cunningham in his Archeological Survey of India Report, when the list of such *rajas* is shown from 1637CE 252 women were burnt alive with the *rajas* of Mandi. Though this practice was legally banned by the Governor General William Bentick in 1829 in India but this practice was still prevalent in different parts of India, including Mandi. G.T. Vigne witnessed the prevalence of the tradition of *sati* during his visit to Mandi in March, 1839 and records that :

> 'One morning my munshi came to me, and told me that a Sati (Suttee), or a widow, who was going to burn herself on the funeral pile of her husband, was about to pass by the garden gate. I hastened to obtain a sight of her. She was dressed in her gayest attire; a large crowd of persons followed her, as she walked forward with a hurried and faltering step, like that of a person about to faint. A brahmin supported her on either side, and these, as well as many around, were calling loudly and almost fiercely upon the different Hindu deities; and the name which was most repeatedly and most earnestly called upon was that of Jaganath; but I do not know whether they alluded to the great idol of Bengal, or to some local divinity.... Her countenance had assumed a sickly and ghastly appearance, which was partly owing to internal agitation, and partly, so I was informed, to the effects of opium, and bang, and other narcotics, with which she had been previously drugged, in order to render her less awake to the misery of her situation. She was not; however, so insensible to what was passing as to be inattentive to two persons in particular, amongst several others who were stooping before her, and were evidently imploring her blessing: they were probably near relations. She was presented at intervals with a plate of moist red colour, in which saffron was no doubt an ingredient, and into this she dipped the ends of her fingers, and then impressed them on the shoulders of the persons who stooped before her in order to be thus marked.'

'In about half an hour the preparations were completed. She was regularly thatched in, upon the top of the pile, whilst her husband's body yet lay outside. It was finally lifted up to her; the head, as usual, and which is the most interesting part of the ceremony, was received upon her lap; the fire was applied in different parts, and all was so quickly enveloped in a shroud of mingled flame and smoke, that I believe her sufferings to have been of very short duration, as she must almost immediately have been suffocated.'

Those at the rear are the earliest of the thirteenth-fourteenth century while the latest *barsela* is of Raja Bhawni Sen who died in 1912 CE. The monuments are valuable for chronological purposes, as fixing with certainty the date of each Raja's demise and the accession of his successor from Hari Sen who died in 1637 CE down to the present time.

Gurudwara Palang Sahib: Mandi has an historical Gurudwara in honour of Guru Gobind Singh, the 10th Sikh Guru, who spent some time in Mandi. The people and the ruler welcomed him with great warmth and supported the Guru in his war against the rule of the Mughal Emperor Aurangzeb; it is said that the city has the Guru's blessings. The Gurdwara is also unofficially referred to as Gurudwara Palang Sahib, because the Guru's Bed 'Palang' is still preserved here.

Shree Deva Ashram: This *ashram* is located in Paddal Mohalla of Mandi town, not very far from Jagannath temple. It is simple single-storied structure with slopy tin roof. It is said that this *ashram* is occupied by one Swami Devi Nand and later by his disciple, Swami Indira Nand for publicising teachings of the Bhagvad-Gita.

Historical Palaces: Mandi is a princely town and there were palaces at the old site of the town, popularly known as *Behras* of Purani Mandi. These were crumbled in the earthquakes of 1905. The palace with four towers known as Chauki was built

Plate 70 : Mandi Palace, side view

Plate 71 : Mandi Palace, side view

by Raja Ajber Sen in 1527 CE. The palaces have received addition and alterations at many times but in different styles of architecture (Plates 70-71). Damdama palace was built during the reign of Raja Suraj Sen, sometimes in 1625CE and has distinctive curved roof usually associated in the hills only with the dwellings of Rajas and gods. The palace has a sizable courtyard. Madho Rai temple occupies the greater part of the lower storey, and it is customary to hold certain state ceremonies in the apartments above it. The rest of the building suffered severely from the earthquake and some of the rooms were hardly fit for habitation. The subsequent restoration to the building including towers have greatly improved its appearance.

William Moorcroft who visited Mandi in the year 1820 observed that :

> 'the most conspicuous object is the palace of the Raja, which stands in the southern part of the town, and presents a number of tall white buildings, with roofs of blue slates, concave like those of Chinese pagodas.'

Vigne informed that :

> 'The palace at Mandi is a long, barrack-like, but not unpicturesque building, with whitened walls, gable-ends, and slated roofs.Before it is a large oak, and the west of it is a garden, in which the Rajah had pitched a tent for me.'

He had further mentioned that:

> 'I partook of the hospitality in a part of palace which had lately been fitted up and painted in the Indian fashion, in fresco, on a snow-white wall.'

There is a legend associated with the palace that the mason who built this palace was given generous rewards by the Raja Suraj Sen and his right hand was cut off with the intention that he may not be able to recreate such buildings.

The Naya Mahal was built by Raja Balbir Sen in 1871 and it was used by the Raja partly as residence and partly as a court. Durbars were also held in it, but a new Durbar hall was built by Raja Bhawani Sen with imposing design in 1906 at the cost of thirty thousand rupees and in 1907, an electric plant was also installed near the palace at the cost of twenty thousand rupees. The construction of the Bhiwani Palace was ordered by Raja Bhawani Sen for his own residence, which was completed in 1911-12 that too after his death. There are multiple courtyards in the complex. The other structures that came up around the palace-complex include the temple, *hawan kund*, Emerson Building, Durbar Hall, Seri Manch and Seri tank, clock tower and Jench ka Naun. The Emerson Building located in the District Court area is now being used as District Library. In front of the palace is the largest Seri Tank with a stone pillar in the middle supporting a lamp. It is said that beneath it is supposed to lie the head of Prithivi Pal, the Rana of Banghal, who was treacherously murdered by the Raja Sidh Sen on his visit to the capital. To placate the ghost the lamp is lit every evening. The walls are built and mounted by railing.

In the year 1927, Raja Bijai Sen built Bijai Palace in the Palace Mohalla across Skodi Khud which was used by the Rajas of Mandi till 1970. The palace has slanting roofs with massive arcades, picturesque facades, royal shrines and sizable courtyards. It has a rich collection of arms and ammunition of the royal family. This erstwhile palace has been converted into a heritage hotel in 1982 and was taken over by the Government.

Baolis: There are numerous *baolis* and springs locally known as Jenchu ka Naun, Pair-re baoli, Sitala and Shyam-re baoli which cater the requirement of water supply in the town (Plates 72-75).

Plate 72 : Baolis at different locations in Mandi

Plate 73 : Baolis at different locations in Mandi

Plate 74 : Baolis at different locations in Mandi

Plate 75 : Baolis at different locations in Mandi

These are mostly located very close to the temples in Purani Mandi and also along the Suketi Khad. Each *baoli* has a wall in local masonry on its periphery with elevated platform for waiting and keeping pitchers. Niches are also provided on the sides for fixing images and in front a paved platform for the purpose of bathing and washing. These *baolis* are also well connected with stepped paths and street lanes.

Anglo-Vernacular School Building: During the reign of Raja Bijai Sen, this school building was built in 1866 to start a new education system in the state under the guidelines of British Raj. The Raja donated a sum of Rupees one lakh for public utility works including establishment of a school in Mandi. In due course under Raja Jogindra Sen, it was raised to double storey at a cost of ten thousand rupees and in 1921 as tribute to the founder of the school, the erstwhile Raja of Mandi, the status of the school was upgraded to high standard and was renamed as Bijai High School after its founder.

Raja Jogindra Sen made several extensions of the building to meet the requirements of various disciplines. Later in 1986, with the introduction of senior secondary classes in Himachal Pradesh, it was renamed as Government Senior Secondary School. The old Bijai High School is a historic wooden structure that has witnessed an unprecedented growth of education for more than fourteen decades but is not in use now. Therefore the old student association of the school has initiated with government for declaration as Heritage Building for the purpose of its preservation and maintenance. This school building appears to have been repaired from time to time. Renovation work is still in progress (Plate 76).

Plate 76 : Anglo-Vernacular School Building

Plate 77 : Heritage Bridge, Mandi

Heritage Bridges: Victoria Suspension Bridge, also known as Victoria Jubilee Bridge connecting Purani Mandi and the new town was built over the Beas River to commemorate the Proclamation Durbar held at Delhi in 1877 at the cost of one lakh rupees (Plate 77). Captain Hoskyns, RE was instrumental in the construction of this airy and light iron bridge. Currently only light vehicles can use the bridge that falls on NH-20.

Another Iron Suspension Bridge was built over the Suketi Khad during the reign of Raja Bijai Sen and this was opened by Sir Dennis Fitzpatrick, the Lieutenant Governor in the year 1894. It has been named after him. This bridge was removed in 1921 and a new pacca masonry one was built in its place.

Bibliography

Berti, Daniela. *Laparoledesdieux. Rituelsdeposs-essionen Himalayaindien.* Paris: CNRS Editions, 2001.

Chanderverkar. 'Temples and Shrines' *in Cultural Forum,* Vol. XIII, No. 3-4, July 1971, Delhi, 1971.

Cunningham, A. *Archaelogical Survey of India Report for the year 1978-79*, Vol. XIV, Delhi, Rep. 2000.

Diserens, Hélène."Lespierresfunérairesde Mandietde Nagaren Himachal Pradesh". *Bulletind'* Études *Indiennes 6:*1988, pp. 201-224.

— "Les yogin'delahautevalléedu Kulu (Himachal Pradesh)" *Bulletind'* Études *Indiennes 9:*1991, pp. 61-73.

District and State Gazetteers of Undivided Punjab, Vol. III, Punjab State Gazetteers, Vol. XII A, Mandi State With Maps, *1904,* Civil and Military Gazette Press, Lahore,1908, Rpt. 1985, Delhi.

Emerson, H.W. *Final Settlement Report of the Mandi State.* Lahore: "Civiland Military Gazette" Press, 1917.

— H.W. *Mandi State. Punjab Gazetteers.* 1920. Vol. XII-A. Lahore: 1920.

Griffin, Lepel Henry. *The Rajas of the Punjab*, Lahore, 1870, Rep. New Delhi, 1977.

Griffin, L.H. *The Punjab Chiefs,* Lahore, 1896.

Handa, O.C. *Temple Architecture of the Western Himalayas,* New Delhi: 2001

Hesse, Klaus. *Staatsdiener, Händlerund Landbesitzer. Die Khatriundder Bazarvon Mandi (Himachal Pradesh, Indien).* Münster: Lit Verlag, 1996.

Himachali, Vinod. *Mandi Rajaon Ki Kahani,* Jalandhar, 1986.

Hutchison, J. and J. Ph.Vogel. *History of the Punjab Hill States,* 2 Vols. Lahore, 1933, Rpt. Shimla, 2000,

Jerath, Ashok. *Hindu Shrines of Western Himalayas,* Jammu, 2001.

Kapoor, M.D. 'Cultural Heritage of Himachal Pradesh' *Souvernir,* Mandi Shivaratri, 1974.

Man Mohan. *History o fthe Mandi State.* Lahore. 1930.

Massy, C.F. *Chief and Families of Note in the Punjab,* Lahore, 1890.

Moorcraft, W.M. and George Trebeck, *Travels in the Himalayan Provinces of Hindustạn and the Punjab* in 2 Vols, London, 1841.

Punjab States Gazetteers Vol. XI IA. Mandi State. 1904. Lahore: 1908.

Punjab State Gazetteers Vol. XII. Suket State. 1904. Lahore:1908.

Ray Chaudhury, P.C. *Temples and Legends of Himachal Pradesh,* Bombay, 1981.

Singh, Mian Goverdhan. *Arts and Architecture of Himachal Pradesh.* Delhi: 1983.

Thakur, Laxman S. *The Architectural Heritage of Himachal Pradesh. Origin and Development of Temple Styles.* New Delhi: 1996.

Upadhyay, Neelmani. *Temple of Mandi* (Monograph), Mandi, 1986.

Vidal, Denis. *Leculte des divinitéslocales dansunerégion del 'Himachal Pradesh.* Paris: 1988.

Vigne, G.T. *Travels in Kashmir, Ladakh, Iskardo, the countries adjoining the mountain course of the Indus and the Himalayas, North of Punjab with map*, in 2 vols, London, 1844.

Vogel, J.Ph. 'The Ranas of the Punjab Hills', *Journal of Royal Asiatic Society, 1908.*

Vogel, J.Ph. 'Triloknath' *Journal of Asiatic Society Bengal,* Vol. LXX, No. 1, Calcutta, 1902.

Index

A

Aitchison Chiefs College, Lahore 26
Alpa Mata temple 30
Amar Singh Thapa 2
Amrit Kaur 27
Anglo-Gorkha war 2, 3
Anglo-Sikh war 3
Anglo-Vernacular Middle School 27
Anglo-Vernacular School Building 141
Ardhanarishvara Temple 39
Ashoka 1
Audumbaras, ancient tribes of Himachal 1

B

Babakot Mandir, Damdama 131
Baba Wasakha Singh Dadehar 4
Bahu Sen 10
Bangleshvari Mahadeva Temple 110
Baolis 138
Barsela Monuments 132
Bhai Parma Nand 4
Bhatanti Mahadeva temple 30, 96
Bhawani Palace 30
Bhimakali Temple 113
Bhutanatha temple 12, 30
Bhuvaneshvari Devi Temple 102
Bijai High School 141
Bijai Sen 141
Bir Sen (765 CE) 10
British Rule 4
Buddhism in Tibet 9

C

Chamunda Mata Temple 116
Chandragupta Maurya 1
Col. A.B. Minchin 26
Coronation Darbar at Delhi 26

D

Damdama Palace 14, 15, 17, 25, 30
Delhi Darbar 24
Dilawar Sen 11
Dugleshvara Mahadeva Temple 86
Durga-Maheshvara Mahadeva Temple 100

E

Ekadasharudra Temple 46
E.M. Atkinson 25

F

Fitzpatrick Suspension Bridge 23

G

General Information 1-8

General Ventura 21
Gorkhas 2
Government Senior Secondary School 141
Govindgarh fort 21
Guptesvara Mahadeva Temple 95
Gurudwara Palang Sahib 30, 135
Guru Gobind Singh 17, 30

H

Hardev Ram 4
Harsha (606-647 CE) 1
Heritage Bridges 143
Hirda Ram 4
Historical Background of Mandi State 9-28
Historical Palaces 135
H.J. Maynard 27
H.W. Emerson 26
Hydro-electric Project at Uhl valley 27

I

Important historical buildings in the Mandi town 30
Indian War of independence 3
Inscription in the Trilokinatha temple 9
Iron Suspension Bridge 143
Ishwari Sen 19, 20

J

Jagannatha temple 30, 123
Jalpa Devi Temple 107, 109
Jodhpur state 24
Jogendra Sen 26
John Lawrence, Commissioner of Jalandhar 22
Jwala Mata Temple 105

K

Kalyan Sen 11
Kameshvara Mahadeva Temple 95
Kamlahgarh fort 14
Kangni Mata Mandir 119
Kangra fort 2
Karanpur forts 14
Karenchana Sen (1278 CE) 10
Kartar Singh Sarba 4
Katoch rulers of Kangra 2
Keshab Sen 12
Kharak Singh 21
Khrisong-detsen, king of Tibet 9
Khua Rani Mandir 118
King Edward VII 24
King Langdharma (900 CE) 9
Kuluta, kingdom of 1
Kunindas, kingdom of 1

L

Lala Lajpat Rai 4
Lomasa Rishi 7
Lord Elgin, the first Viceroy of India 23
Lord Kitchener 26
Lord Mayo, the Viceroy of India 23

M

Madho Rai 14
Madho Rai Temple 123
Mahadeva Neelakantha Temple 74
Mahadeva Temple 59
Mahakala Temple 92
Mahamrityunjaya Temple 63
Maharaja Ranjit Singh 2
Maharaja Sansar Chand 2

Mahishasuramardini Mandir 119
Mahmud Ghazni 2
Mandav Nagar 6
Mandi Municipal Committee 27
Mandi State 11, 26, 28, 29, 30
Man Singh, the Raja of Guler 14
Mata Chintapurni Temple 99
Mathura Singh 4
Mian Bir Singh 16
Monumental Remains of Mandi 29-143
Monuments 132
Moropant Pingle 4
Mughal dynasty 2
Muslim invaders 2
Muslim invasions in northern India 2

N

Narayan Deo of Hurang 12
Narayangarh fort 12
Naya Mahal 30, 138
Neelakantha Mahadeva Temple 69

P

Padmasambhava (750-800 CE) 6, 9
Panchavaktra Temple 37
Parashar temple 10
Parkash Dei Mandir 119
Prithivi Singh 13

Q

Queen Mary's College, Lahore 26
Quit India Movement of 1942 4

R

Radha-Krishna Temple 120
Rai Rajeshvari Devi Mandir 119
Raja Jagat Singh of Nurpur was 13
Raja Ram Sen 14
Raja Sansar Chand Katoch 18
Raj Mahal 30
Ramachandra temples 30
Ramalingeshvara Mahadeva Temple 71
Rana of Gandharb 11
Rana of Sagrur 11
Ranas of Kamlah 11
Raneshvara Mahadeva Temple 66
Ranjit Singh 19, 20
Ras Behari Bose 4
Ravi valley 17
Revolt in 1857 3
Ron suspension bridge 23
Rupeshvari Devi Mandir 119

S

Sanatan Dharma Sabha 126
Shahpur fort 14
Shaiva Shrines 30
Shakti or Devi Shrines 96
Shamsherpur fort 14
Shamsher Sen 18
Shiva-Deula (Bijali-Mahadeva) temple 43
Shivaratri festival 7
Shiva-Rudra Temple 56
Shiva Temple 76, 78, 83
Shree Deva Ashram 135
Shyama Kali temple 15, 30
Shyam Sen 15
Siddh-Bhadra Temple 53
Siddh Ganapati Temple 129
Siddh-Kali temple 30, 80
Siddh Sambhu Mandir 29, 80, 90
Sikandar Lodi 2, 11
Sikh Chieftains 18

Sikh Darbar 22
Sir Charles Rivaz 25
Sir Dennis Fitzpatrick 23
Sir Douglas Forsyth 23
Sir Henry Davies 23
Sir Louis Dane 26
Sir Robert Egerton 23
Sir W. Mackworth Young 23
Sitala Mata temple 30, 96, 118
Sita-Rama Radha-Krishna Temple 121
Small Monolithic Temple 89

T

Tarna Mata or Shyama-Kali Temple 111
Tibetan tradition 9
T.P. Gillmore 26
TrilokinathaTemple 34
Trilokinatha temple inscription 11

V

Vaishnava Shrines 30, 120
Viceregal Darbar at Lahore 27
Victoria Jubilee Bridge 143
Victoria Suspension Bridge 24, 25, 143

W

Wazir Gosaon 24
William Moorcroft 20, 137

Y

Yashodhan Singh 27

Z

Zalam Sen 20